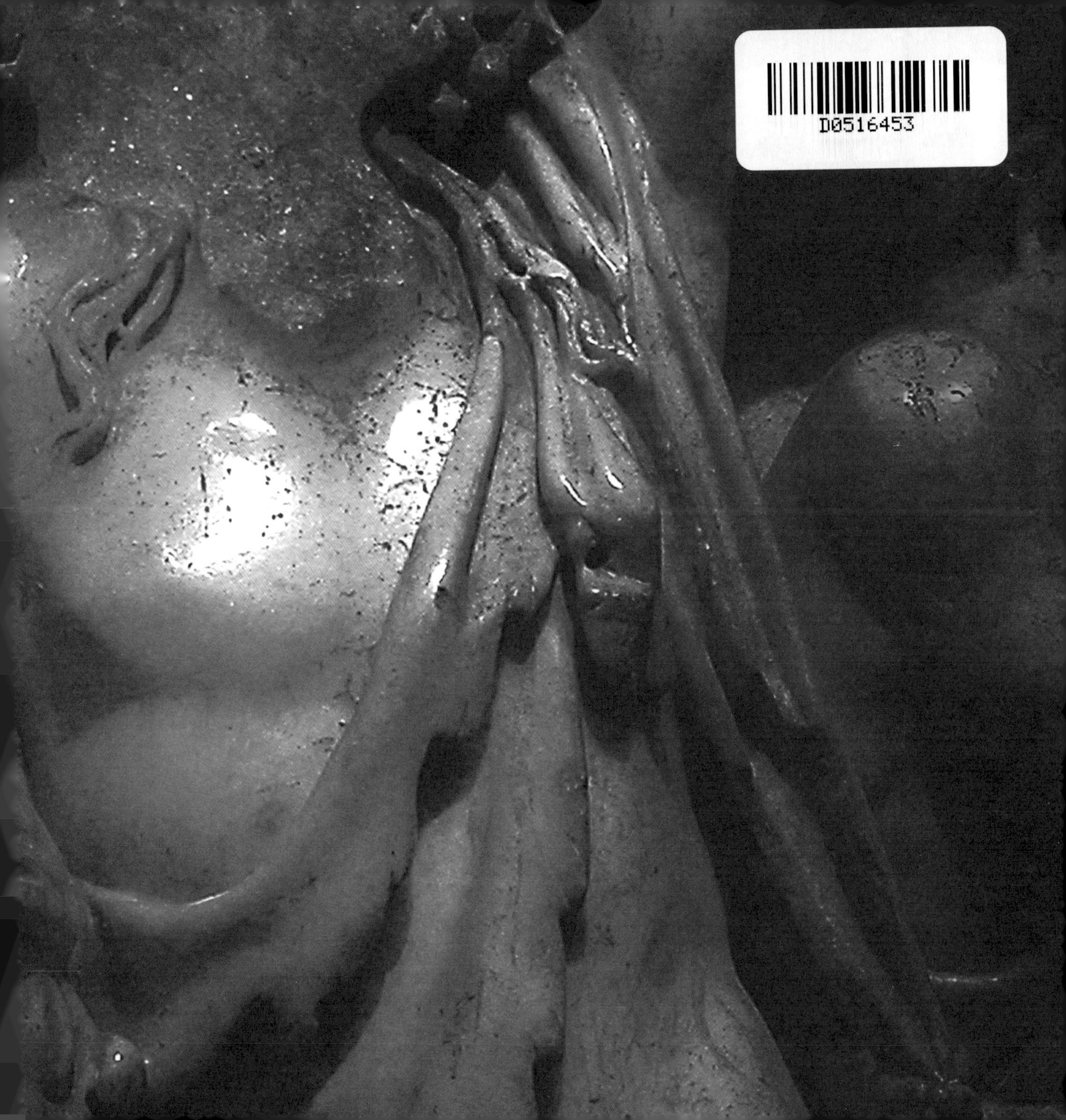

THE MIRROR OF LOVE

the Mirror of Love

ALAN MOORE
JOSÉ VILLARRUBIA

foreword by
ROBERT RODI
introduction by
DAVID DRAKE

TOP SHELF PRODUCTIONS
ATLANTA / PORTLAND

The Mirror of Love

Text Copyright © 1988, 2004 by Alan Moore

Illustrations © 2004 by José Villarrubia

Introduction © 2004 by David Drake

Foreword © 2004 by Robert Rodi

Published by Top Shelf Productions, Chris Staros and Brett Warnock, PO Box 1282, Marietta, GA 30061-1282, USA. Top Shelf Productions® and the Top Shelf logo are registered trademarks of Top Shelf Productions, Inc. All Rights Reserved. No part of this book may be reproduced without permission, except for small excerpts for purposes of review. Visit our online catalog at www.topshelfcomix.com. First Printing, February, 2004.

Printed in Singapore

Library of Congress Cataloging-in-Publication Data

Moore, Alan, 1953-
    The mirror of love / Alan Moore ; illustrated by José Villarrubia ; foreword by Robert Rodi ; introduction by David Drake.-- 1st American hardcover ed.
                        p. cm.
    ISBN 1-891830-45-7 (cloth : alk. paper)
    1. Homosexuality--History. 2. Gay men--History. 3. Lesbians--History. 4. Bisexuals--History. I. Villarrubia, José, 1961- ill. II. Rodi, Robert. III. Drake, David, 1963- IV. Title.
    HQ76.25.M663 2003
    306.76'6'09--dc22
                                                    2003024486

Edited by Chris Staros
Logotype designed by Nancy Ogami
Book design by José Villarrubia and Paul Ryan
Copy editing by Robert Venditti

To anyone who loves, a kiss, with tongues and everything.

—Alan

To Mel Odom, whose beautiful and brave work gave me permission to start dreaming.

—José

TABLE OF CONTENTS

FOREWORD

When *The Mirror of Love* first appeared in 1988 it was the cornerstone of *AARGH!* (Artists Against Rampant Government Homophobia), a comics anthology specifically assembled to counter Britain's proposed antigay Clause 28 (see Appendix IV). *AARGH!* was remarkable in that it featured an A-list of comics creators speaking out for a cause (gay rights) that was at least as incendiary, if not more so, than it ever had been. Gay activists, having made some concrete gains, had alarmed and galvanized the opposition against them; and the AIDS crisis gave that opposition a new cudgel to wield.

AARGH! was the product of Alan Moore's own Mad Love Publishing, and as such it's fitting that his contribution was, thematically, the most ambitious. In my review of the work in *The Comics Journal* #126, I called *The Mirror of Love* "an attempt to distill the entire history of homosexuality to serve as the subtext to a sustained love affair between two hermaphroditic angels, mirror images of each other." In this new edition, the angels — along with Steve Bissette and Rick Veitch's original illustrations — are gone, replaced by a series of ravishing photographs, by José Villarrubia, that stand as a highly personal essay on their own.

What remains from the work's original incarnation is (again from my review) "a poetic rhythm that allows it to move effortlessly from Sappho to Shakespeare to Joe Orton," in a way that is "exquisitely moving — not because it's a testament to same-sex love, but because it's a testament to love, period." It's unusual for a political polemic to merit reading fifteen years after the fact. Much of what provoked *The Mirror of Love* into being is no longer quite so relevant — for while gay rights is still a contentious issue in much of the western world, gay people, gay stories, and gay ideas have entered the cultural mainstream in a way that would have been unimaginable in 1988.

But in this new presentation, unmoored (excuse the pun) from *AARGH!*, we can see that *The Mirror of Love* isn't a polemic at all. It is in fact an attempt to dwarf politics with the imposing edifice of history, culture, and art. It stands as some kind of victory that it's still here, inciting us to think and feel, while Clause 28 seems so very far away — and in its grotesqueness, almost quaint.

Robert Rodi
Chicago, 2003

INTRODUCTION

Over the course of our twenty-year friendship, José Villarrubia has brought many things to my life. From the summer we met as teenagers in Baltimore, Maryland, in 1982 — José a student of art and me of theater — we've shared something as close to parallel lives as I've experienced in my forty years on the planet. As José's creative trajectory went from student to artist to teacher, alas, so did mine. After college, José chose to remain in Baltimore to build his life, while I ventured to New York City. Through the years we have continued to share it all — often over the phone. He has been my confidant, my accomplice, my sounding board, my brother. As a witness to his journey, I feel blessed and honored that José has brought me his questions and his counsel, his troubles and his triumphs, his gossip, his laughter, his family, his fears, his constantly curious intellect, his unquenchable compassion for others, his unbeatable zest for life. And in January 1998, José brought me something else. Something that would — thrillingly, surprisingly, and necessarily — become a turning point in our lives. He brought me *The Mirror of Love*.

It was a Sunday afternoon. The phone rang. I expected it might be José, as he and I had been chatting quite regularly on the weekends for the past couple of months, each of us recovering from romances that had ended with an especially painful pair of broken hearts. (Again, parallel lives.) I answered. It was José. And indeed, he was near tears. Not, however, over the broken heart stuff, but rather from a piece of writing called *The Mirror of Love*. As José explained, its curious title was borrowed from an unpublished frontispiece by British

Decadent illustrator Aubrey Beardsley. It was intended for a book of poems by his rumored lover Marc-André Raffalovich, and it was censored for featuring a hermaphroditic angel. The text that José had found in an esoteric magazine called *Rapid Eye* was written by a revered British writer, and told the story of the legacy of same-sex love. Tentatively, José asked if he could read it to me. Keen to the impact the piece was obviously having on José, I said, "Yes, please. Let's hear it!"

With care, José proceeded to read to me *The Mirror of Love*. After tangling through some of the more obscure references in the text, while listening to José give a gentle determination to the words he was so enamored with, I too found myself becoming as intoxicated with the richness of the piece as José was. After he finished, there was a pause. We breathed. Then José said, "I think it should be a monologue. There's a little one-act theater festival coming up here at Baltimore's Theatre Project for Gay Pride in June. It's called Queer Cafe. And I think," he seemed to gulp, "I would like to perform it there. Would you direct me?"

Now, José may be an artist, but unlike millions of people who fantasize about jumping up on stage, José has never harbored show-biz aspirations. And so for him to want to take that risk — and take this piece to an audience — was obviously coming from a deep need within. The one that, akin to finding love for the first time, makes you want to run into the streets and shout it out to the world, "Love! Love! I found love!" What José had found, as you will understand when reading this book, was a meditation as profound as the birth of "first love" — a meditation on its wily, undying survival: Eternal Love.

Considering our mutual mending of hearts at the time, the sudden emergence of *The Mirror of Love* couldn't have been more timely. The adaptation was more than just an interesting project for José and I to throw ourselves into. Rather it would become an opportunity to re-focus the loose energies of romance at hand and use them to create a piece of art in order to heal, renew, and move on.

This realization didn't occur to either of us automatically. Nor should it have, really. At the time, the two most important elements of the project were clear. First, José's commitment to performing it. And second, the appropriateness of José's instinct that *The Mirror of Love* actually belonged on stage. Like him, I recognized its innate theatricality immediately. It was language-driven. It had wit. It had ideas, drive, and passion. And, of course, it had all those delicious odes to the famous (and infamous) of homo history (something that José and I both savored). Moreover, there was a rhythm and cadence in the writing that screamed out: Speak me! Sing me! I will intoxicate the audience!

Later, as I studied the text, I grew to appreciate the subtle nuance and sharp economy with which Moore had written *The Mirror of Love*. The way he threads the work with historical detail, without ever losing grip of the fierce, emotional fuse that burns throughout, is astonishing. In the months that followed, as I read more of his work, I found that this was true of all of Alan's writing. From comic books to performance art, Alan was clearly a poet of tremendous power.

José, of course, already knew this. As a life-long consumer of comic books, José had been a fan since he first discovered Moore's *Swamp Thing* series in 1985. From there, José devoured everything Alan created — *Watchmen*, *V for Vendetta*, *Miracleman*, *Batman: The Killing Joke*, *Big Numbers*, *Lost Girls*, *A Small Killing*, *Brought to Light*, *From Hell*, as well as his critically acclaimed novel *Voice of the Fire*.

Meanwhile, timing and grace were on our side in bringing *The Mirror of Love* to the stage. José secured an invitation to perform the piece in Queer Cafe. All we needed now was the author's consent.

Now, José had never met Alan. Locating his address in England, José blindly wrote to Alan and told him about our idea to realize *The Mirror of Love* on stage. There was no answer. We got a little nervous. As the clock ticked, we decided to chance making a call.

The phone rang. Alan answered. In a deep, resonant voice, shaded with his marvelous Northampton accent, Alan couldn't have been more gracious. He thought it was an intriguing idea to set *The Mirror of Love* on stage as a monologue. (Later I found out that Moore, who had himself ventured into live performance to explore ideas, believed that, in a theater, magic and art are more or less analogous. "Both are the creation of something out of nothing," he has stated.) By the end of our conversation Alan had given us his blessings and, artistically, completely set us free: "Do whatever you think is best," he said.

With the writer's approval, and the performer's confidence, I went full ahead with my idea for directing the adaptation — though not without error. In fact, I went about it completely wrong. Still, if José and I hadn't headed down that initial road, I doubt you'd be holding this book in your hands.

In real life, because José teaches art in college — and because the text contained so much historical data — I envisioned *The Mirror of Love* as an academic lecture with slides. Not only did I believe it would be a natural segue for José in making his stage debut, but, with the assistance of the images, I also saw the opportunity to visually isolate and underline pieces of the story, pointing out their cultural significance to the audience.

Doable and logical? Yes. Emotional? No. In order to give this version texture, context, and conflict — so that, emotionally, I could steer the actor and audience to reach *The Mirror of Love*'s dramatic conclusion of passionate reaffirmation of eternal love — I envisioned José would be playing a character that was an aging professor, sadly and melancholically giving his final lecture.

Ugh. Looking back, I recognize it was a terrible choice. But for nearly a month we went with it, not realizing the idea wasn't the ideal setting for the monologue.

In the process, José scoured the Internet and ransacked the library in search of images that identified the dozens of characters and stories mentioned in Alan's text. Suddenly, myriads of zip files packed with jpegs entered my e-mail box each day. There were scans of Oscar Wilde, Judy Garland, Alan Ginsberg, and the Stonewall riots intermingled with paintings by Michelangelo and etchings depicting Sappho, the Canaanites, and those ever-elusive Ladies of Llangollen. José was overjoyed with his findings. I was overwhelmed. Somewhere in the middle, however, we were both learning an important visual history that would become a foundation from which we would continually draw on our way to giving *The Mirror of Love* its stage life.

Residing in different cities, José and I mapped out a series of rehearsals that would alternate between weekend visits to New York and trips to Baltimore. As we prepped for our first weekend of "play practice," José called with a concern. He'd spoken with a mutual friend about the adaptation. Our friend, who was also a visual artist, fidgeted, frowned, and finally said, "It sounds kind of sterile. Don't you think the piece is really all about sex?" Suddenly, it hit me: to make it play on stage, the story of *The Mirror of Love* wasn't about visualizing the details in the text, it was about visualizing the action in the text: making love. Within minutes, José and I had re-evaluated the adaptation and knew that what was taboo, what was the central conflict, what centuries of homo oppression had really been all about was the sensual, simple, romantic act of two people of the same sex making love. Any stage adaptation of *The Mirror of Love* had to reflect that. Scrapping the lecture concept, I began to imagine José on stage with a partner, a lover — in the post-coital confines of a bed. From the center of Alan's writing I pulled an idea. "Darling do not weep. 'Twas just a dream." Yes, I thought, a dream. On stage it could all be just a dream:

a monologue spoken from the vast, Jungian swirl of the collective unconscious, one lover to another.

Partially inspired by the catalogue of images José had e-mailed me, I knew the stage had to appear as scrumptious and lush as possible — a dreamscape mesh of Caravaggio, Michelangelo, and Hockney. Of course, since the performers were playing lovers, they had to be found in bed. And nude. Behaviorally, it was natural. Visually, it was classical. Being a trouper (with a thousand hours of life study drawing classes under his belt) José agreed without trepidation. And immediately joined the gym.

Over the four months that we rehearsed the piece, our intensity to give Alan's story to an audience grew inward, as well as outward. The project attracted some invaluable creative energy. Along with José's fierce discipline to technically hone his voice, emotions, and storyteller's sense of logic and charm into the text (a necessary element for a monologist), we asked a brilliant young composer named Chris Mandra, a graduate from Baltimore's Peabody Conservatory of Music, to create an original score for the piece, and engaged a deeply gifted performer named Michael Willis to play José's sleeping lover. (While José hovered about the stage telling the story of *The Mirror of Love*, Michael lay nude on a bed, covered in a white, silken parachute. Silently and eloquently, Michael shifted, stretched, and coiled — the night moves of a dreamer.) In the end, aided by a lighting design which seemed to echo the sensations of dark, gathering clouds — found sifting through the boundaries of heaven and hell — the production was everything I could have hoped for. Audiences and critics were dazzled by the complexity and scope of the text and its presentation.

As director, my job had been to usher the story on to the stage while staying as true to the author's original intent a possible. Doing so with *The Mirror of Love* was certainly a privilege. However, once the audience settled into their seats and the lights came up on the stage, my job was over. And the telling of the story belonged solely to the actors. Suddenly, all the prepping and rehearsing, the tweaks and the tech, the notes, adjustments, and blocking assignments vanished — and the magic arrived. For, to paraphrase Alan, when an actor takes charge on stage it appears as if he is creating something out of nothing. Indeed, that is what happened when José took *The Mirror of Love* to a live audience.

But that's not where José's desire to tell the story of *The Mirror of Love* stopped. Bringing Alan's text to the stage had breathed fresh life into its legacy. Allowing it to dwell in the utterly public forum of a live theater had certainly been thrilling and tribal. But, as is the nature of the medium, it had also been temporal. For all who experienced our stage adaptation, *The Mirror of Love* is now but a memory. However, over the years, still deeply enriched by his theatrical experience, José began to contemplate a more lasting version of *The Mirror of Love*. Something that would keep the story as alive as it had been on stage. Something that could once more be given to an audience — if only an audience of one. Something you are holding in your hands right now.

Indeed, the richness of José's love for the richness of Alan's story has continued, as *The Mirror of Love* has now gone from page to stage and back. And while much inspiration was drawn from his initial research (in both my misguided ideas for adaptation, as well as the images and ideas we came up with for its final theatrical presentation), one of José's greatest sources of guidance came from the panel descriptions of the images as Alan envisioned them for the original comic book version. Still, there is another element that inhabits each and every image. It is a personal one: the uniqueness of José's imagination. It is the element that, when I direct a play, I cannot completely supply to the performer. It is the element that must come from within him. It is the magic.

At Baltimore's Theatre Project, in the summer of 1998, José delivered that element in spades. And now, like the actor who led us through the story on that stage — swirling us from emotion to emotion as he guided us from word to word, painting the pictures in the air with his voice, body, and soul — José once more takes charge to lead us on Alan Moore's journey through the looking glass, to reflect the power and passion that is *The Mirror of Love*.

David Drake
New York City, 2003

THE MIRROR OF LOVE

Even preceding landfall,
things loved freely once,
ignoring gender.

Blind desire
made pond-slime fish,
turned fish to apes with sex
life's glorious engine,
churning in the mud.

The animals remember:
dolphins still rotate
their matings
between their own sex
and its reverse,
their raptures echoing
for miles.

On land,
the first societies,
great herds of she-beasts,
raised their young together,
without males,
whose part in reproduction
was unknown.

The women licked
and groomed each other
with men watching,
circling, circling round…

In the beginning then,
three million years
of motherhood.

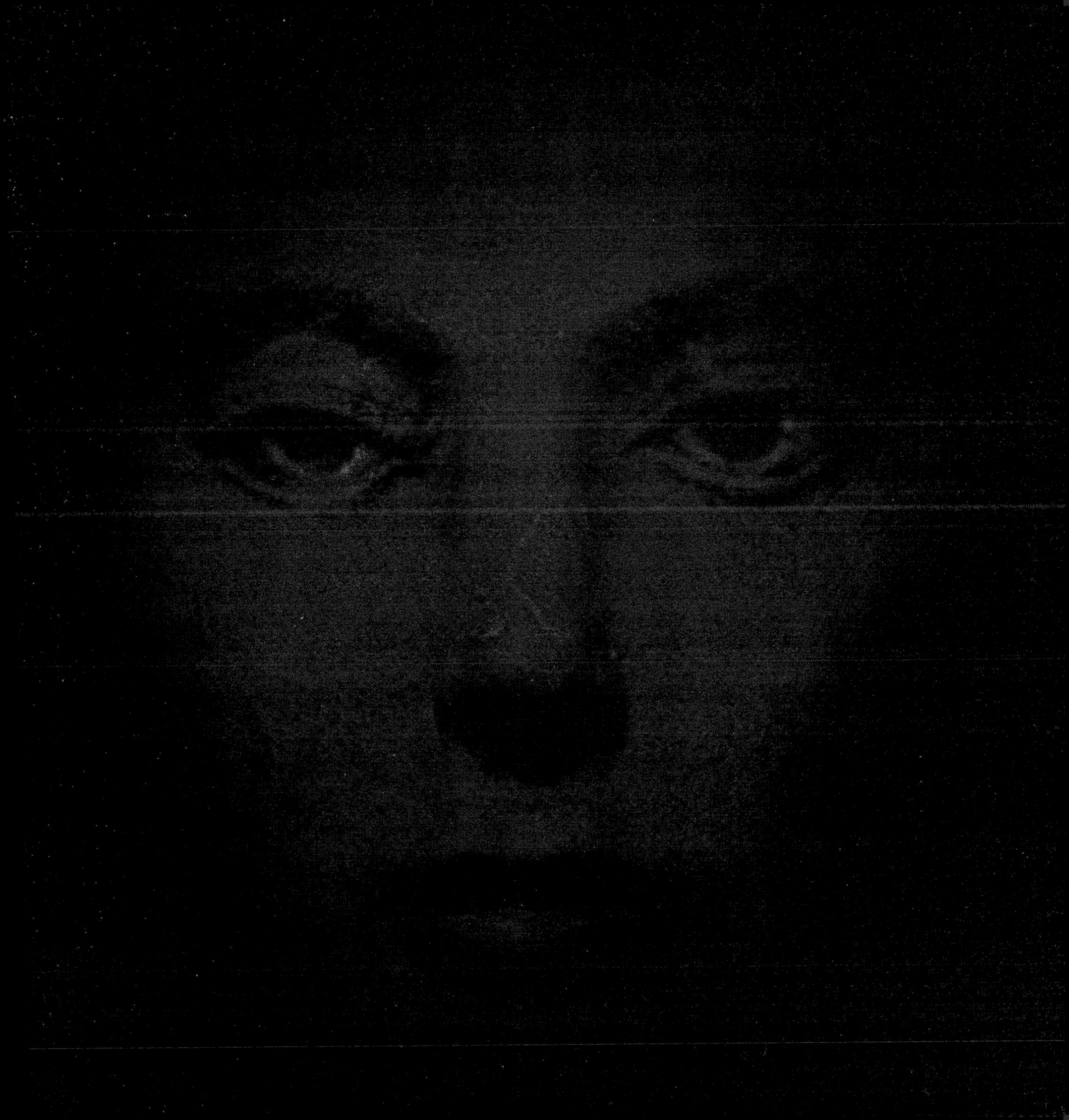

The Word
came later,
and the word
was power,
was patriarchy:
firstborn children
squirmed on altars
of a father god.

The word
was law:
in Sumer,
women scorning men
had teeth crushed
with burned bricks.

Law,
once conceived,
applied to everything.

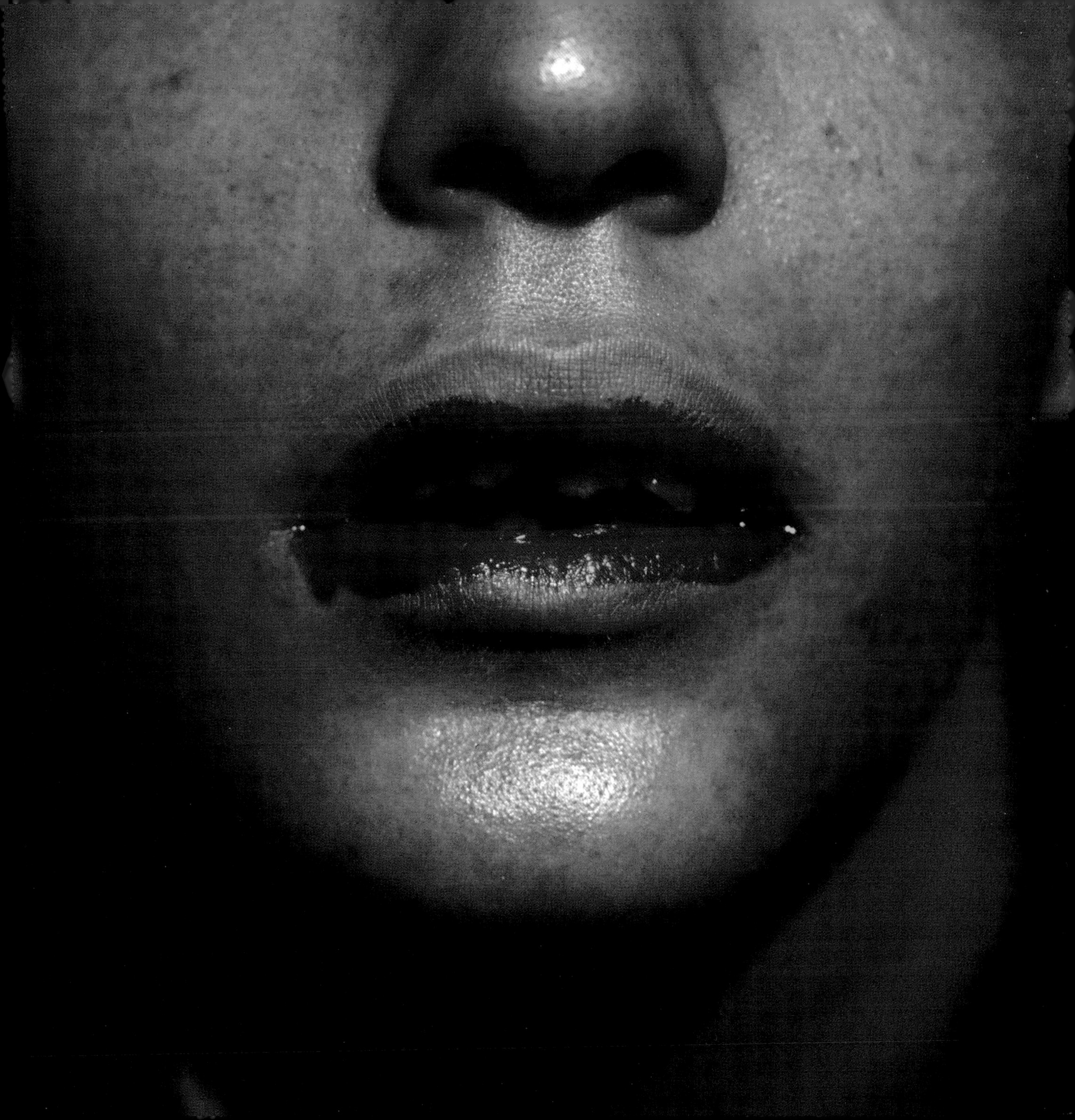

Leviticus condemned
most sexual practice
as unclean,
including that
between two men.

This was designed
to snub the Canaanites,
whose male priests
practiced sodomy.

Had they been
cannibals instead,
how different
might things be.

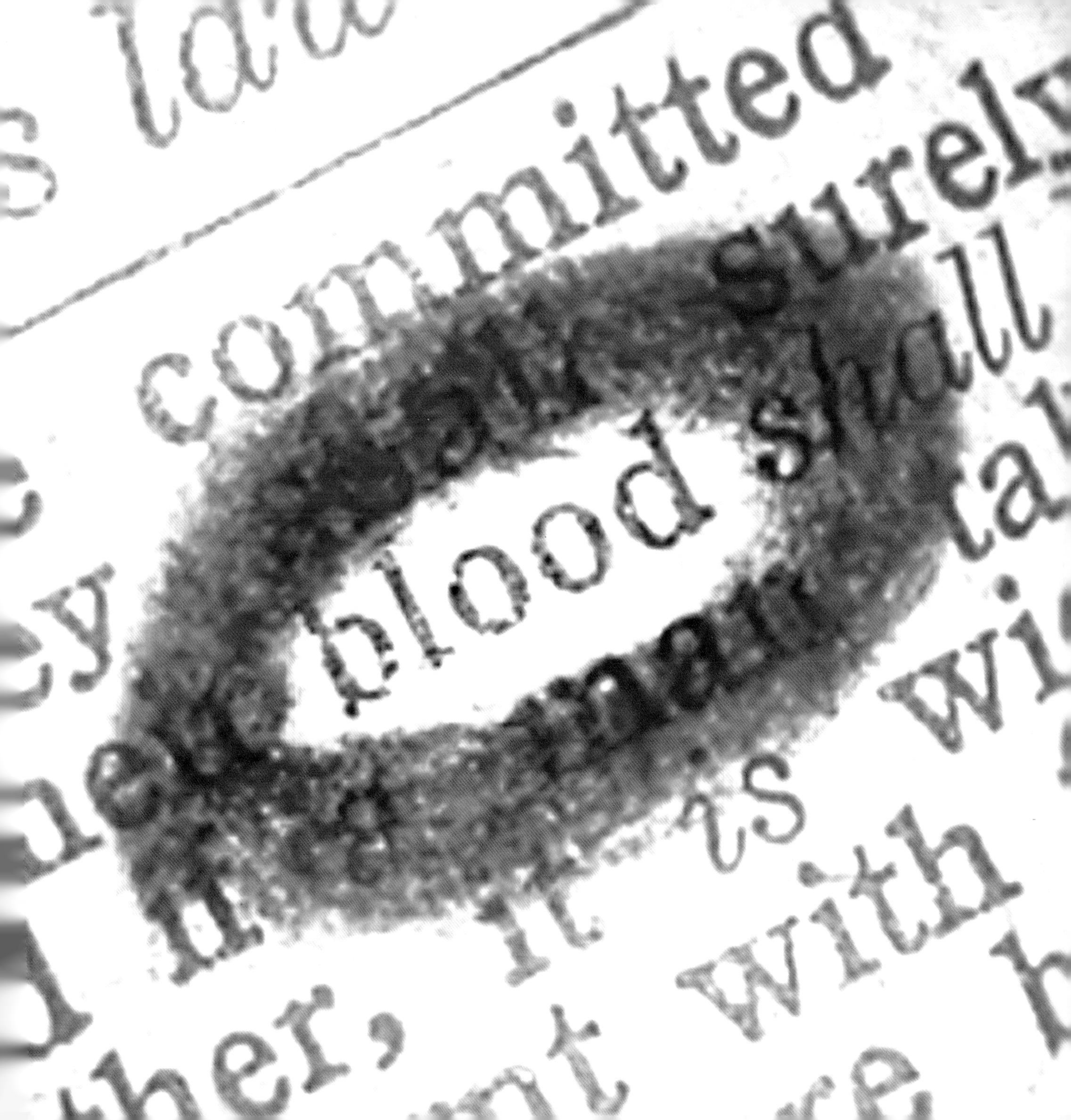
committed
blood shall
man
it is
with
her,

We gasped
upon Devonian beaches,
huddled
under Neolithic stars.

Spat blood
through powdered teeth,
staining each other
as we kissed.

Always we loved.

How could we otherwise,
when you are so like me,
my sweet,
but in a different guise?

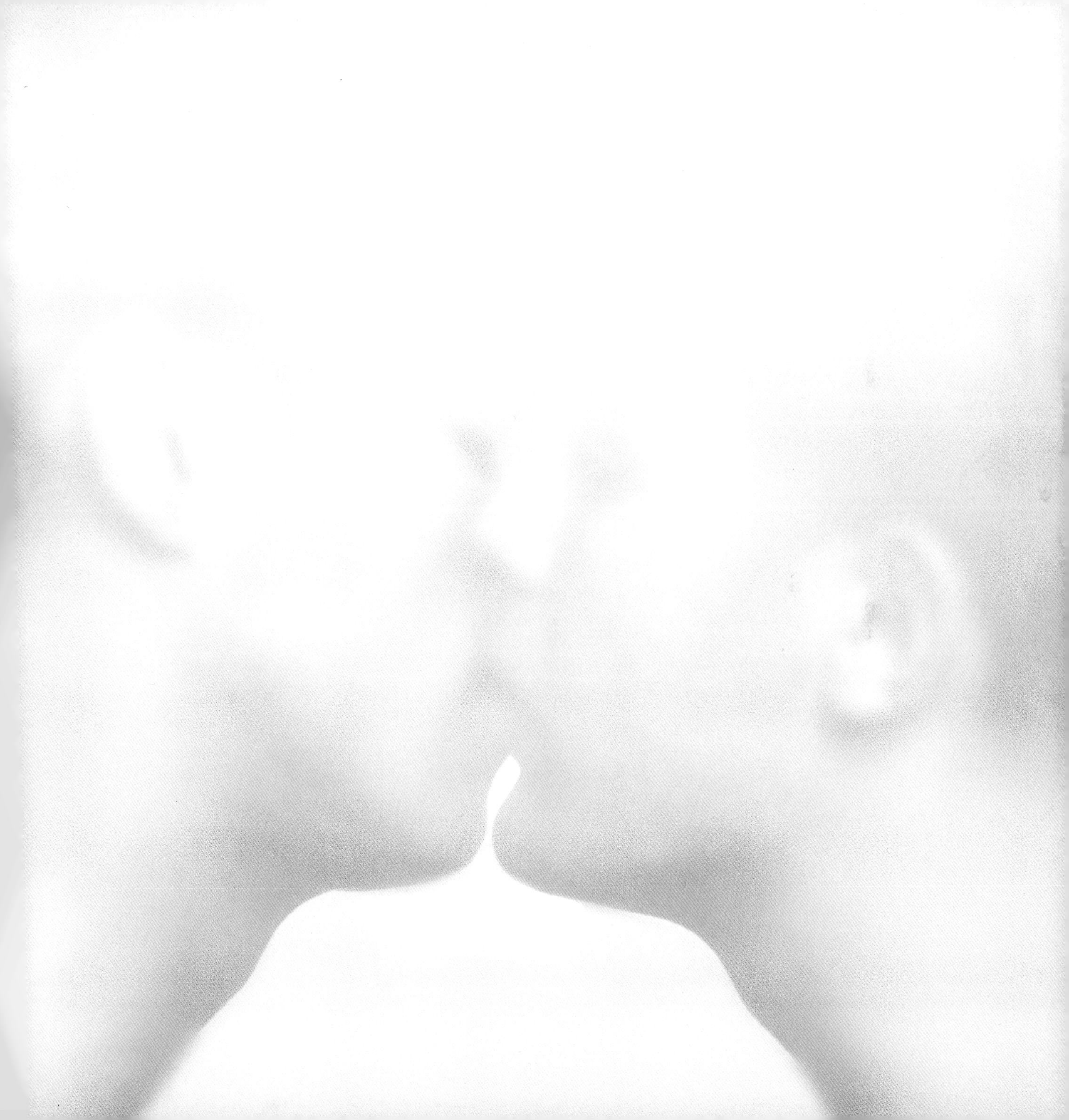

We loved
while great Mediterranean
cultures flourished,
their homoerotic urges
troubling them
not at all.

Regarding man-boy
love as civilized,
the Greeks and Romans
made it thus a badge
of class and rank
within their careful
edifice of power.

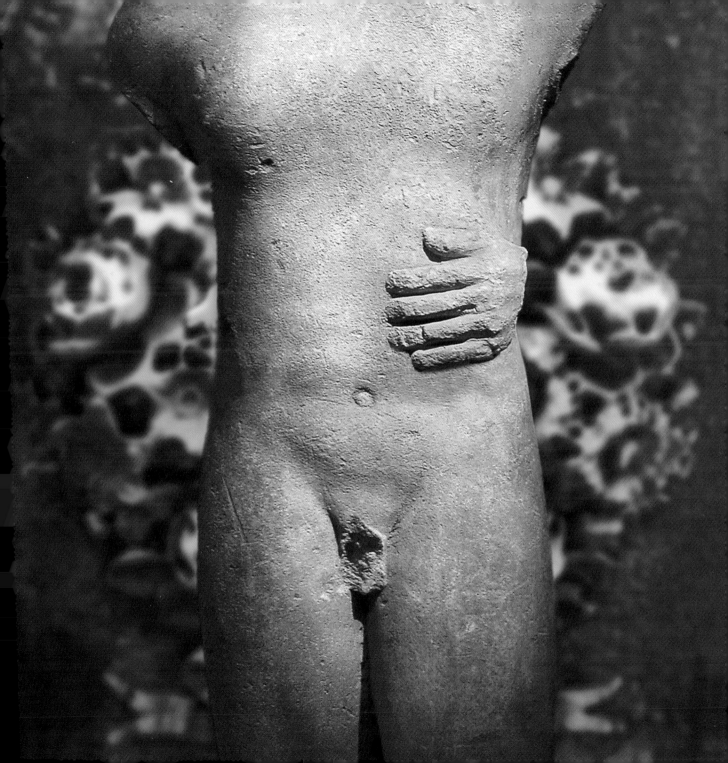

The Spartan army
 ventured further:
male love
was enforced,
producing soldiers
who'd defend
their frontline lovers
to the death.

Demanding tougher breeds,
they exposed infants
to the elements,
particularly girls.

Perhaps because of this,
by the time Rome invaded
there were only sixteen
Spartans left.

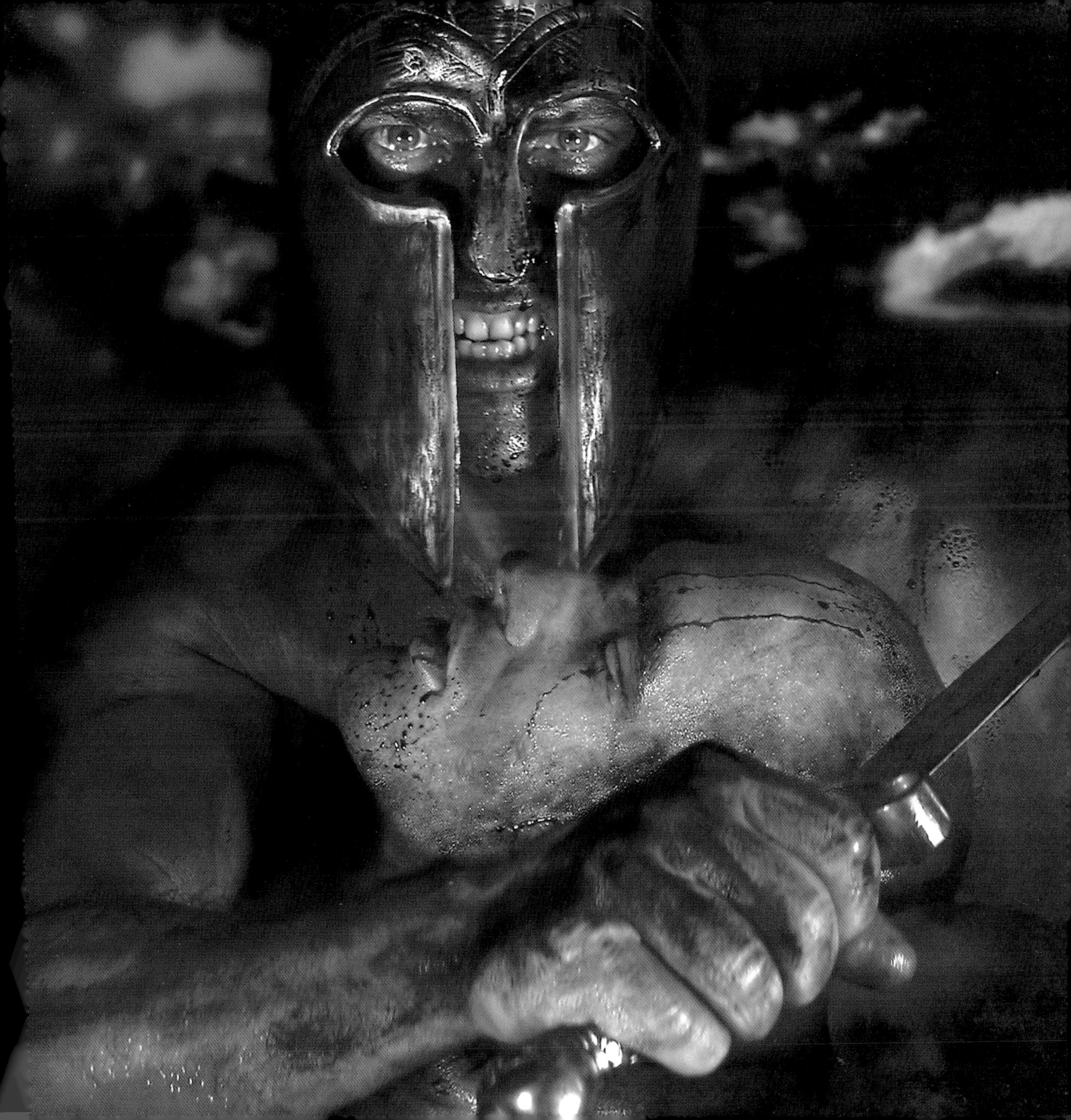

Corinth's transvestite
troops aside,
this usage
was unique.

We were creators:

Homer sought in verse
to hug Achilles' shade,
while on her isle,
exquisite Sappho
reminisced of myrrh
poured on her lover's head;
of girls upon soft mats
with all they most desired
beside them.

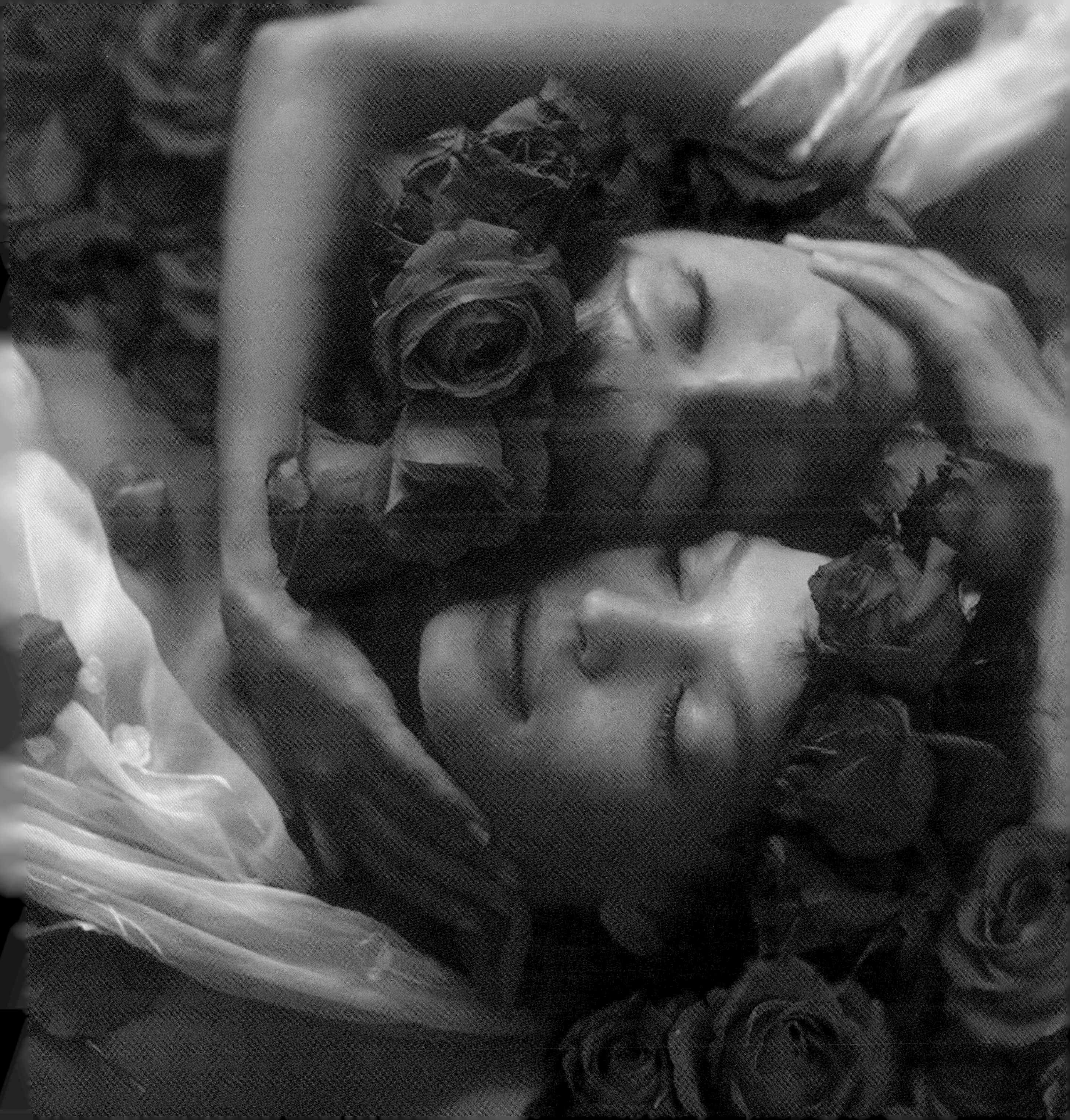

Yet this tolerance
could not endure
the rise of Christianity,
which quite ignored
Christ's love for outcasts
and instead embraced
moral severity.

Defining sex as base,
an obstacle to faith,
St. Paul named
same-sex love,
for the first time,
as sin.

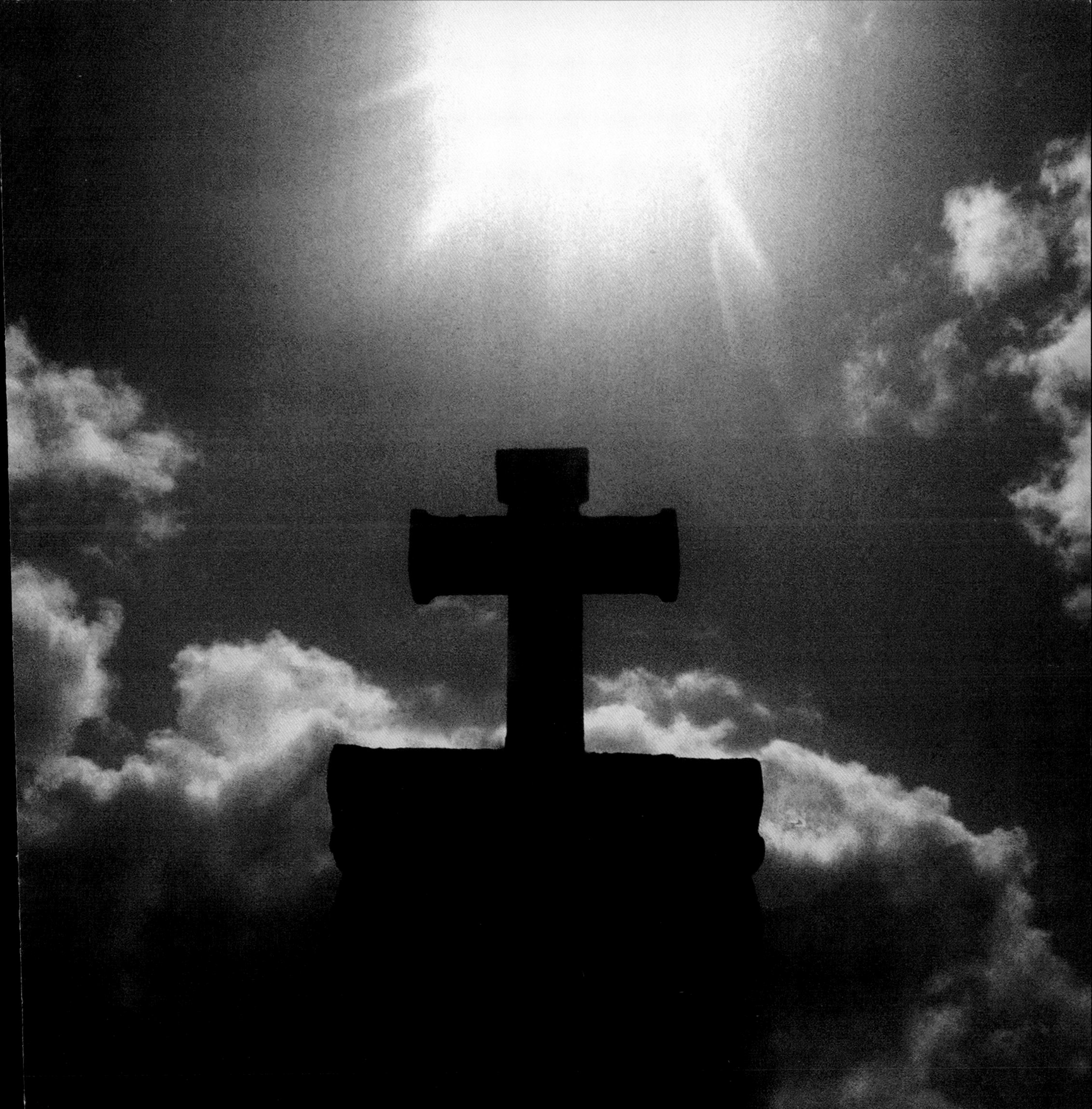

Ah, sin.

Was that its name,
which stole a kiss
behind the interlocking
shields of war?

Sin that made
Sappho weep
and write,
'I have not had
one word from her?'

With baby-blood
upon their hands
they saw our love
and named it sin.

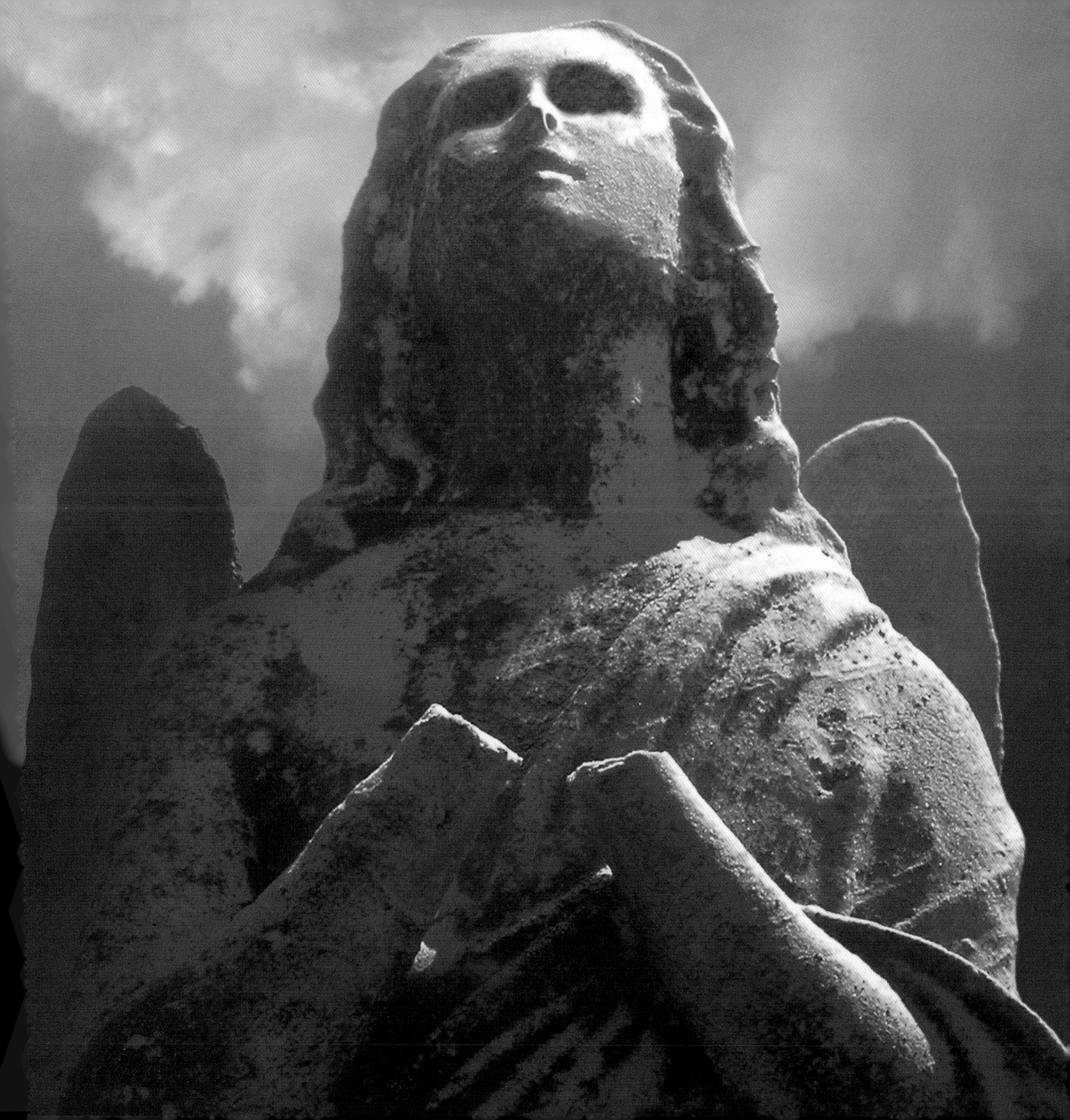

Thomas Aquinas,
by the 13th century,
had systemized
degrees of vice,
including copulation
with an undue sex.

Since in the high dark ages
such pronouncements
were quite readily
made law,
burnings occurred;
beheadings;
bodies twisting
slowly in the breeze.

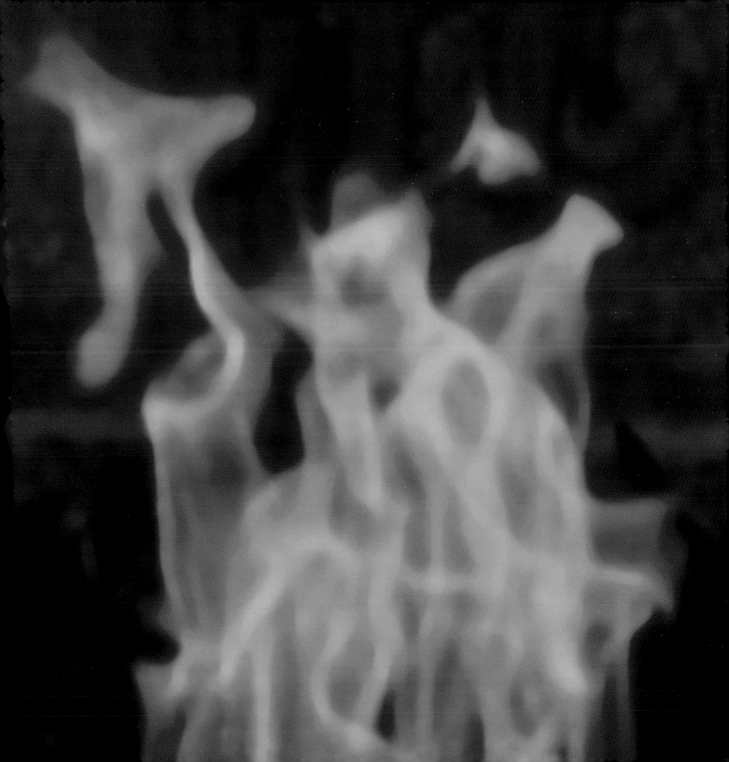

Although to hang
for sodomy alone
was rare,
such charges loaned
vendettas weight.

Knights Templar,
charged with sodomy,
had instead pressed
Philip of France
for debts
he couldn't pay.

The Pope,
owing Philip in turn,
arranged the Templars'
persecution.

Then, as now, our love
was used conveniently
as a smear.

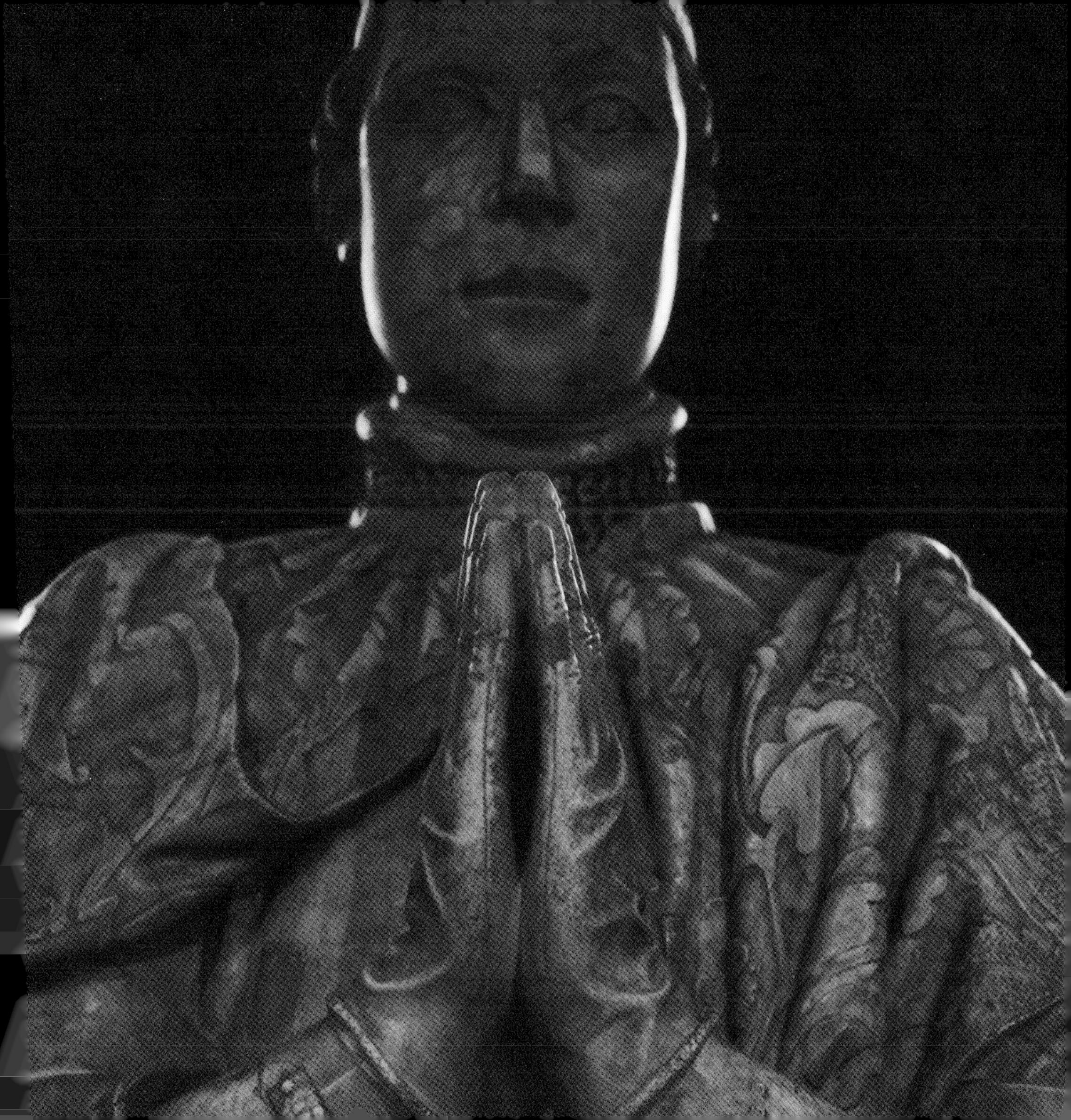

As the Renaissance blossomed,
cities gradually returned,
and in their alleys
our subculture thrived,
a pale, night-blooming flower.

Despite church savagery,
an improved social clime
once more
brought forth
our Muse.

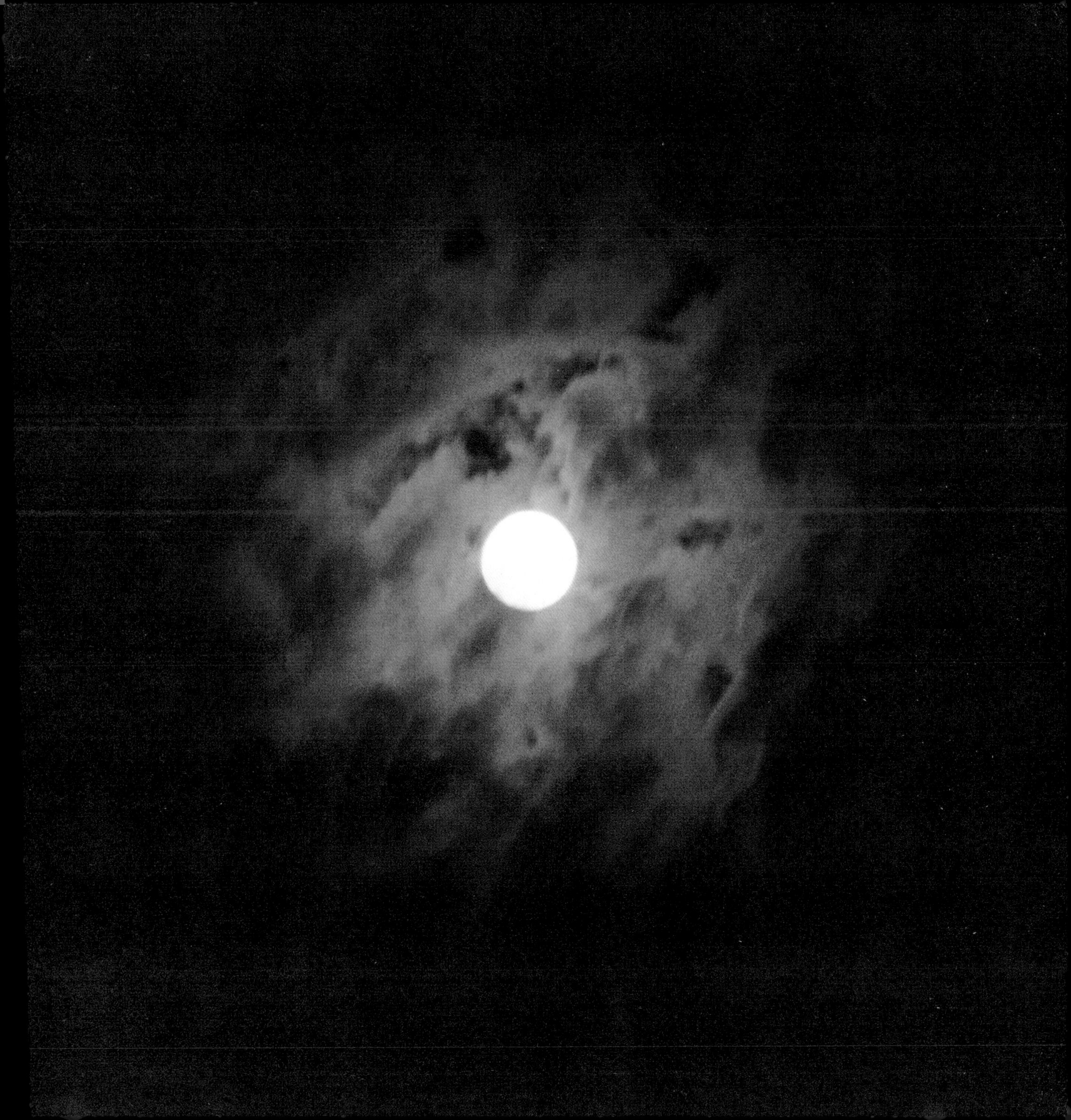

Thus, Michelangelo
gazed heavenwards
into a crowded Sistine sky
and told his dear Tommaso
that though vain,
malignant hordes attribute
what their grosser wills obey,
yet should
this love,
this faith,
pure joys afford.

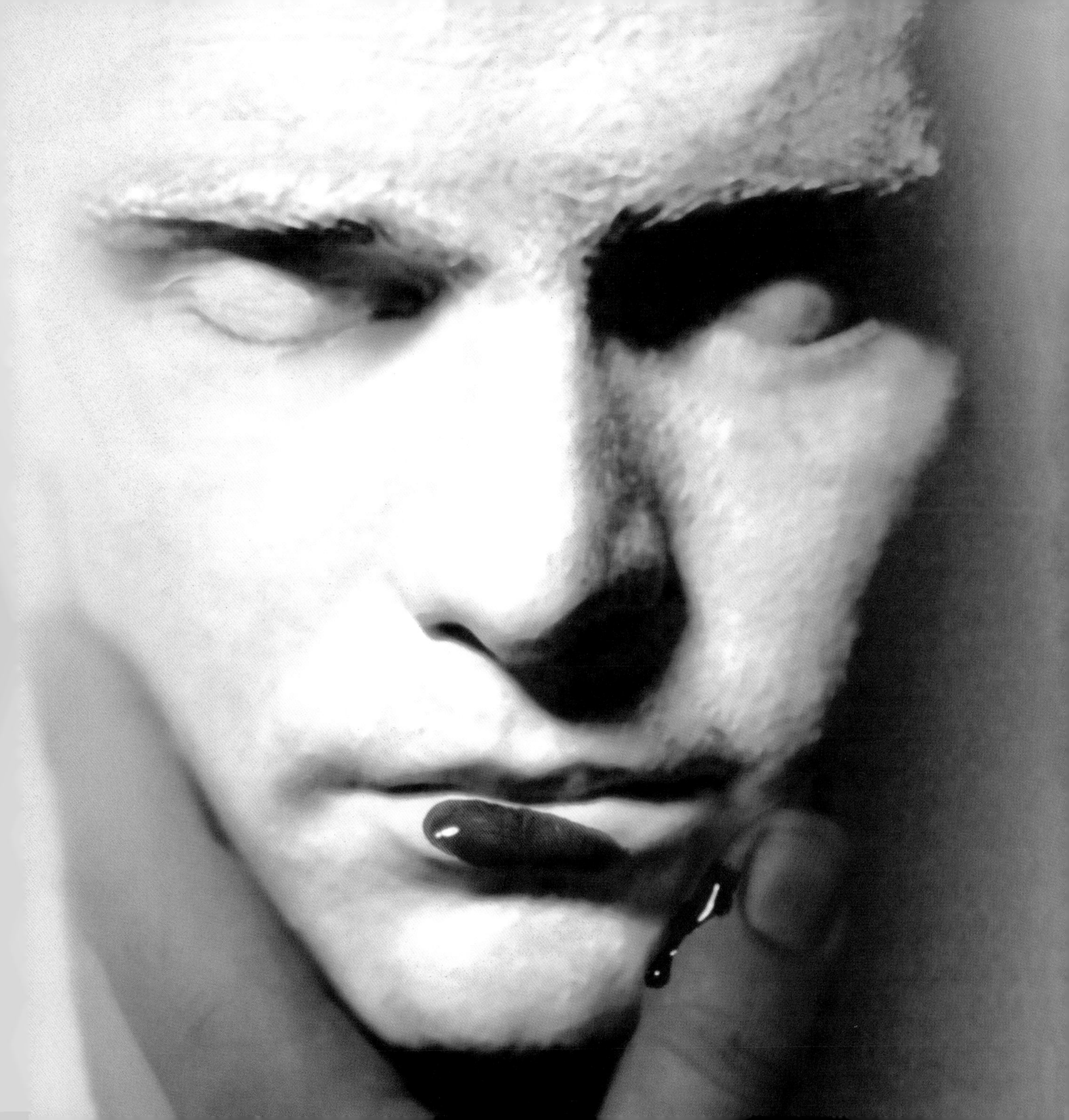

How could he know,
upon his palette there,
creating heaven
from a hell
of cramped discomfort;
chisel trembling
on the brink of freeing
David's shoulder
from chill rock?

How could he know
what trials the future held,
how gross its will?

My love,
the vain, malignant hordes
are with us, with us still.

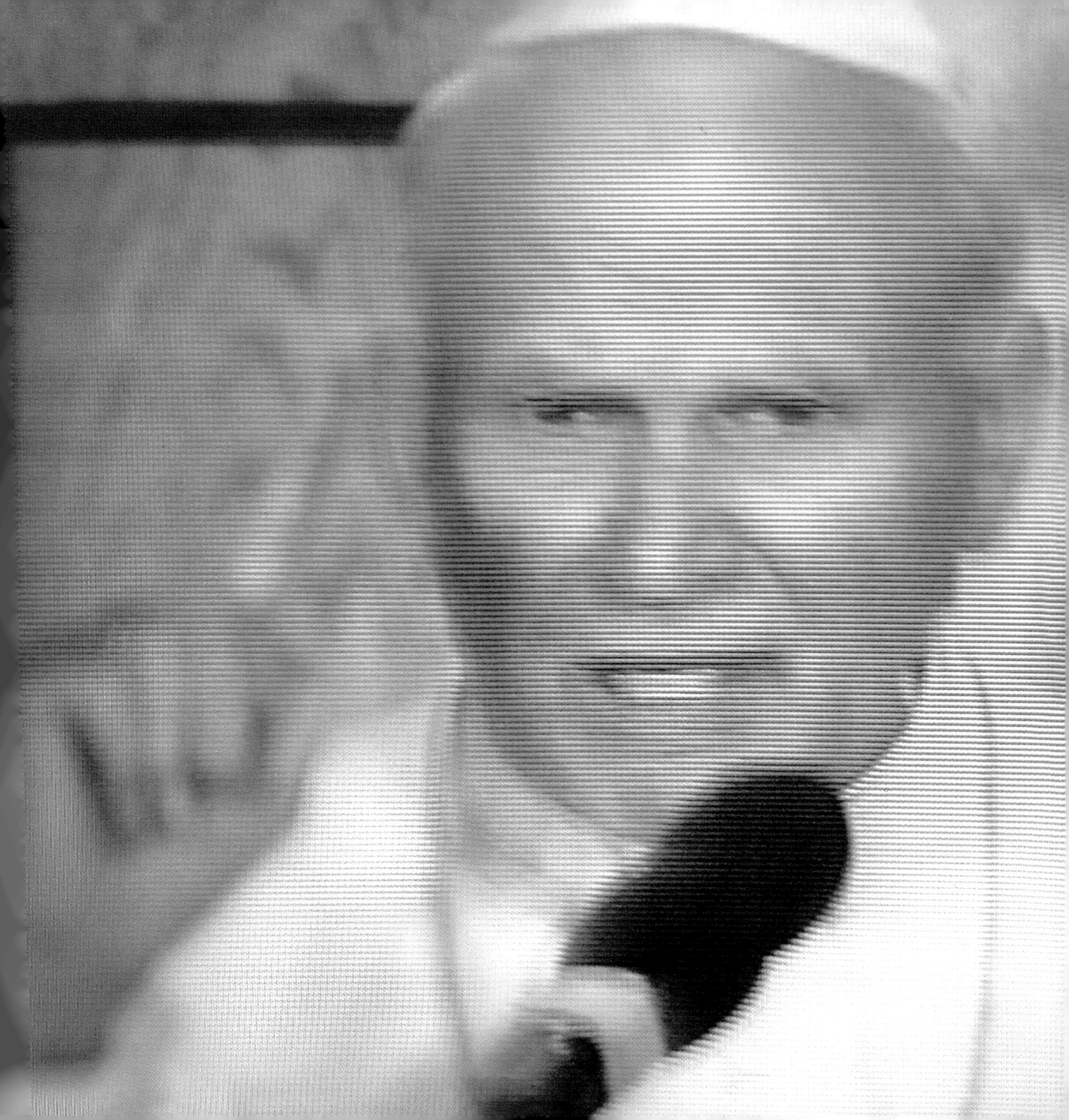

The 16th century favored
cross-dressed men
in women's roles,
forging a bond
between our culture
and theater
that endures today.

That era's greatest dramatist,
in sonnets to
his benefactor,
Mr. W. H.,
proclaimed his love
more ringingly
than he portrayed
the ruin of dynasties.

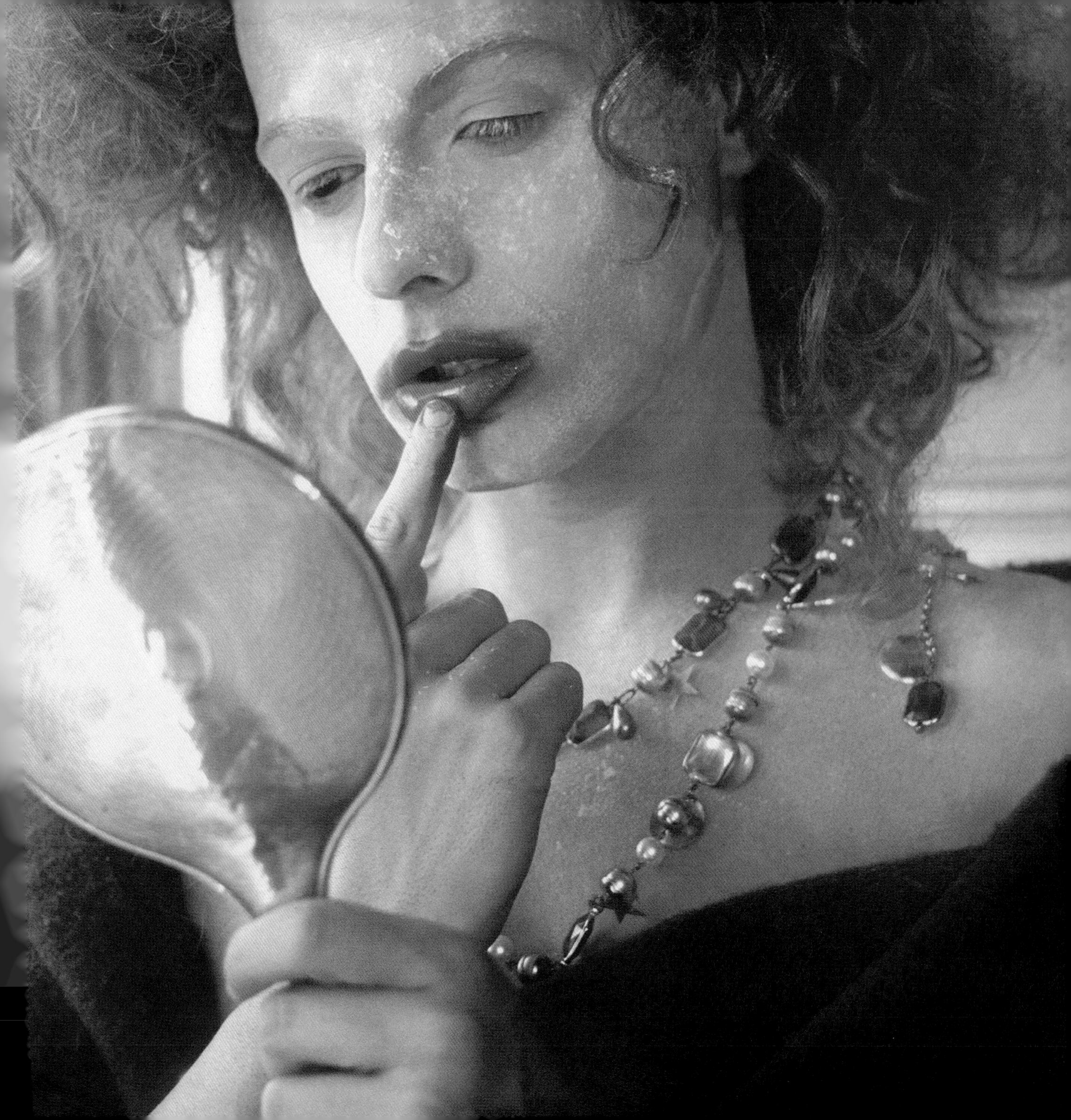

In time such 'friendship,'
passionately expressed,
became the custom,
and society, having
no great desire to punish
what was then
a harmless commonplace;
having no word
for homosexuality,
could draw
platonic veils
across our love,
and look away.

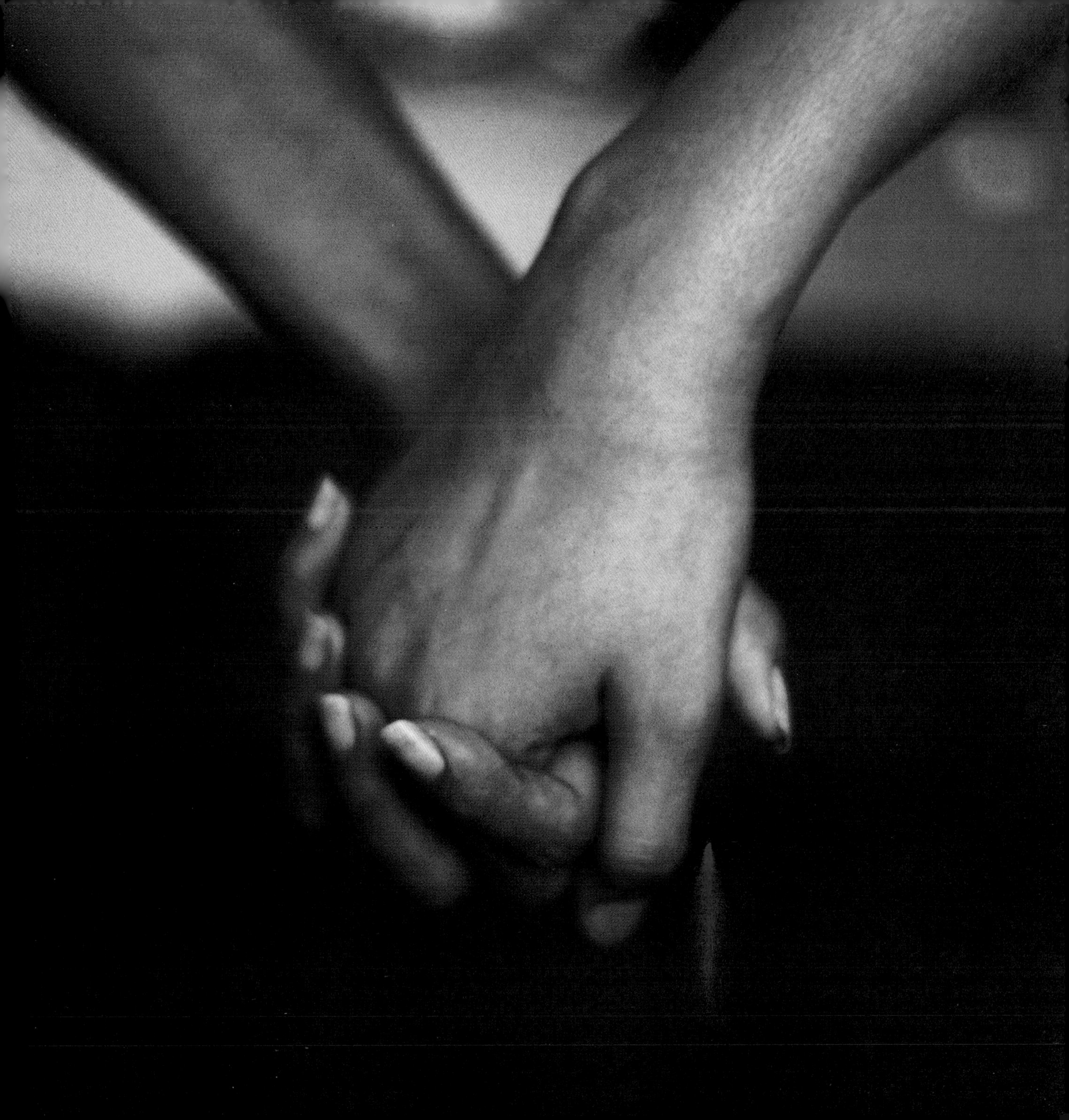

Nowhere was this more evident
than with the Ladies of Llangollen,
women living openly together
in eccentric isolation,
objects of suspicion,
yet also of fascinated awe.

Amusing in their tantrums,
cherishing the picturesque,
they scattered rosebuds
round their cottage,
banished Wordsworth
when he slighted it in verse.

Without them,
history's diminished.

We grew, but in obscurity.

Emily Dickinson described
her lover's breast
as fit for pearls,
her words unread,
her voice unheard
'til she was dead.

Amidst his dust-tanned voice
Walt Whitman dream'd
a new City of Friends,
builded from tender glances
in the hired-hand scrum.

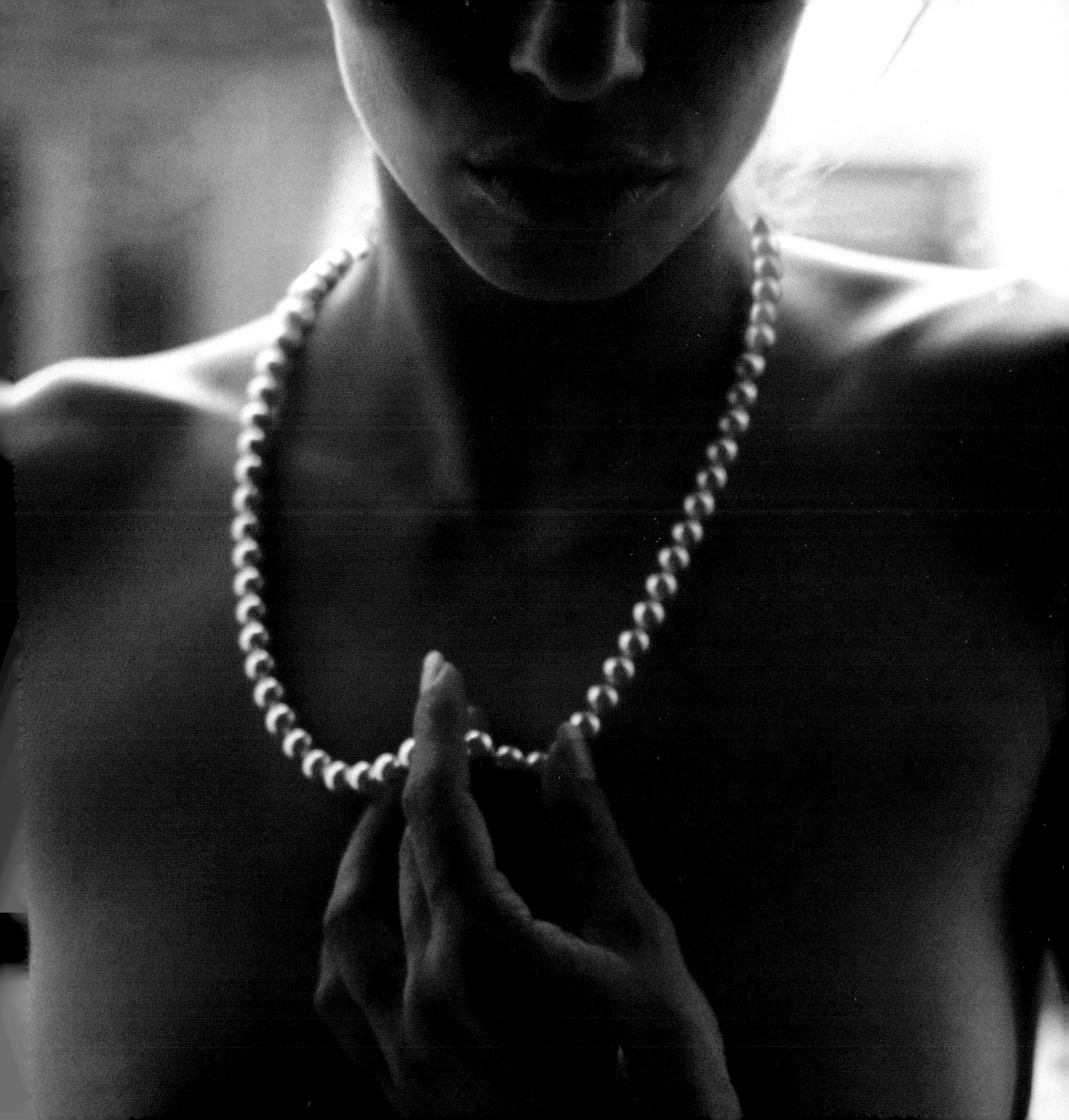

So Shakespeare dipped a quill
into his troubled soul,
while Eleanor and Sarah
fired their servants
and nailed poems to trees.

On Emily's pure heart,
her lover's weight a night…

Who'll care, my love?

Who'll guard
such fragile gems as these?

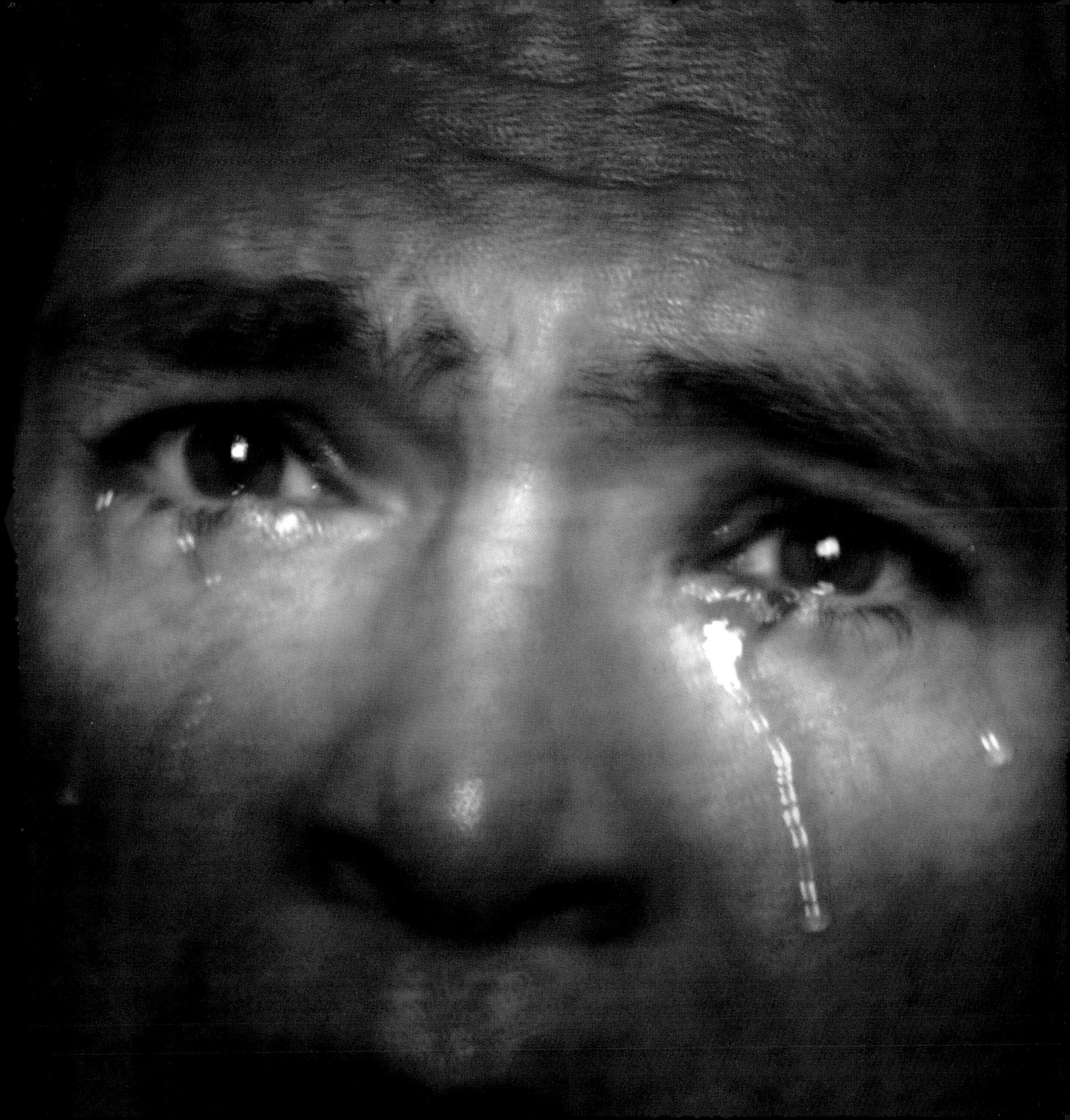

Only within enlightened cultures
could we breathe:

Natalie Barney's salon
scandalized and entertained,
where Gertrude Stein took tea
and Mata Hari, naked,
rode jeweled stallions.

Outrageous Natalie,
who, spurned by Renée Vivien,
delivered herself in a satin coffin
to the poet's door,
while Paris smiled.

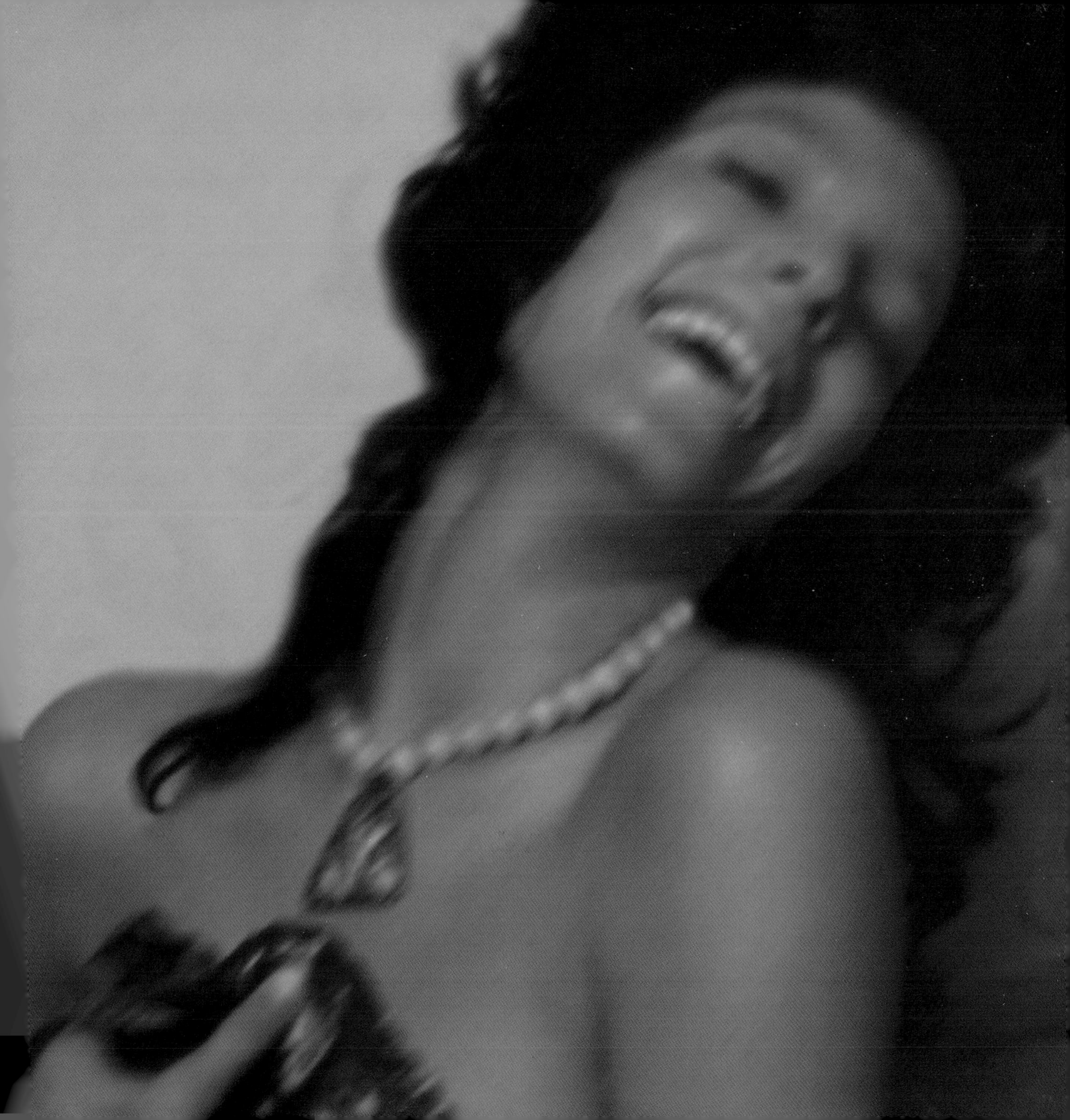

Elsewhere,
in Leipzig, 1869,
one K.M. Benkert
first referred to
'homosexuality.'

Industrial England's view
that all might be
explained by science
prompted doctors
to declare us
merely ill,
not friends
or sinners
after all.

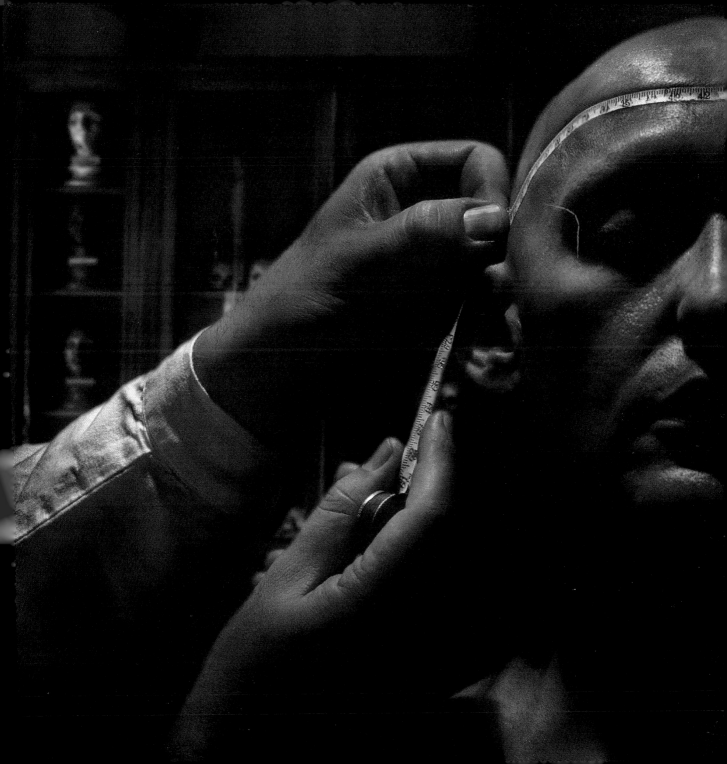

The molly-houses
rattled in the wind.

The climate changed,
as Oscar Wilde learned
to his cost, too fond
of working lads;
of feasting with panthers.

His beloved's father, a marquis,
denounced him as a sodomite.

Pressing for slander, recklessly,
Wilde was exposed,
condemned to Reading Gaol
then exiled in disgrace.

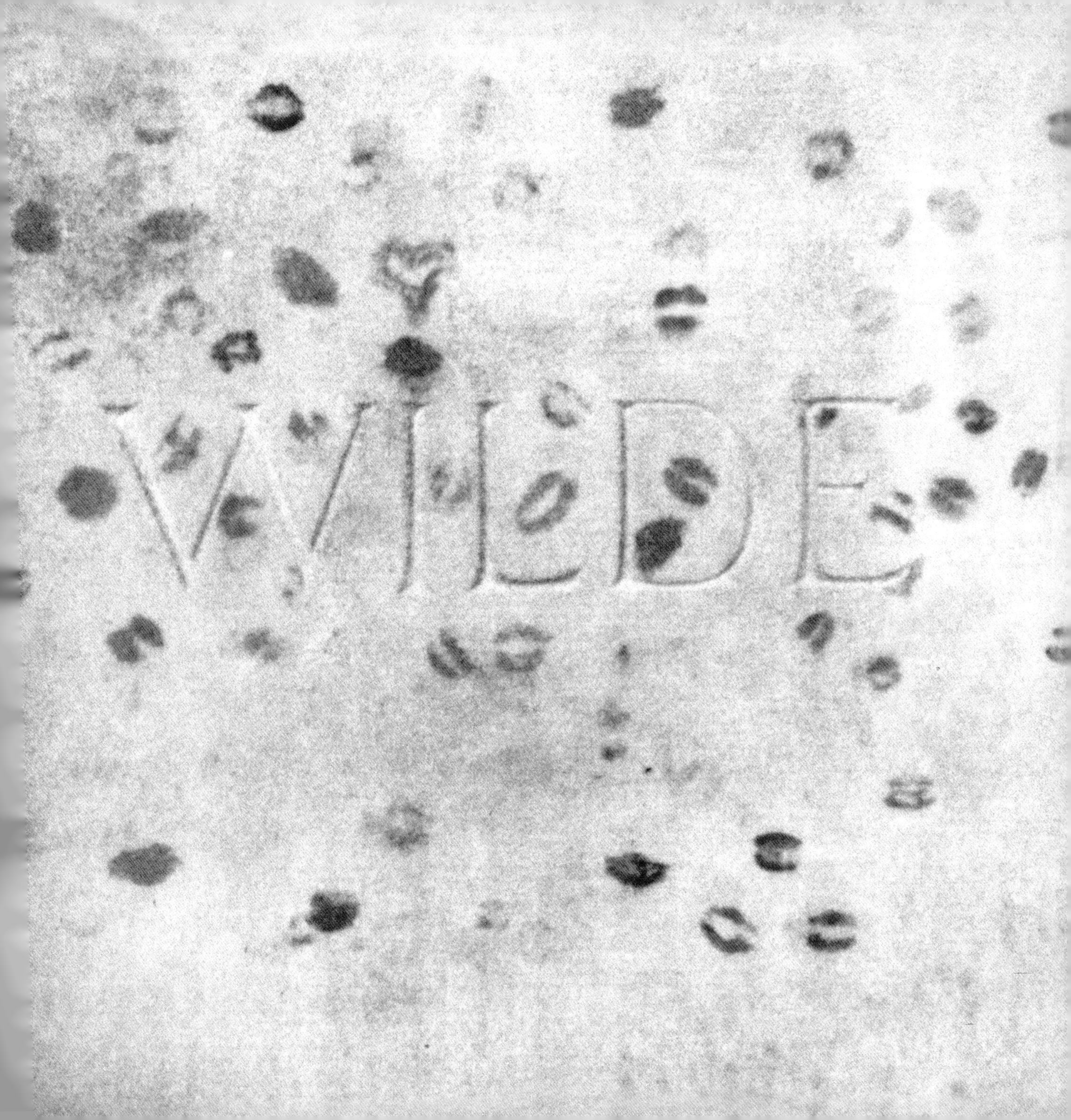
WILDE

The era closed
with Wilde's mauve nineties
fading to gray,
and yet contained the seeds
of something proud, humane:

From Germany,
before the century's end,
came the first protests
against laws on sodomy.

Emancipation had begun.

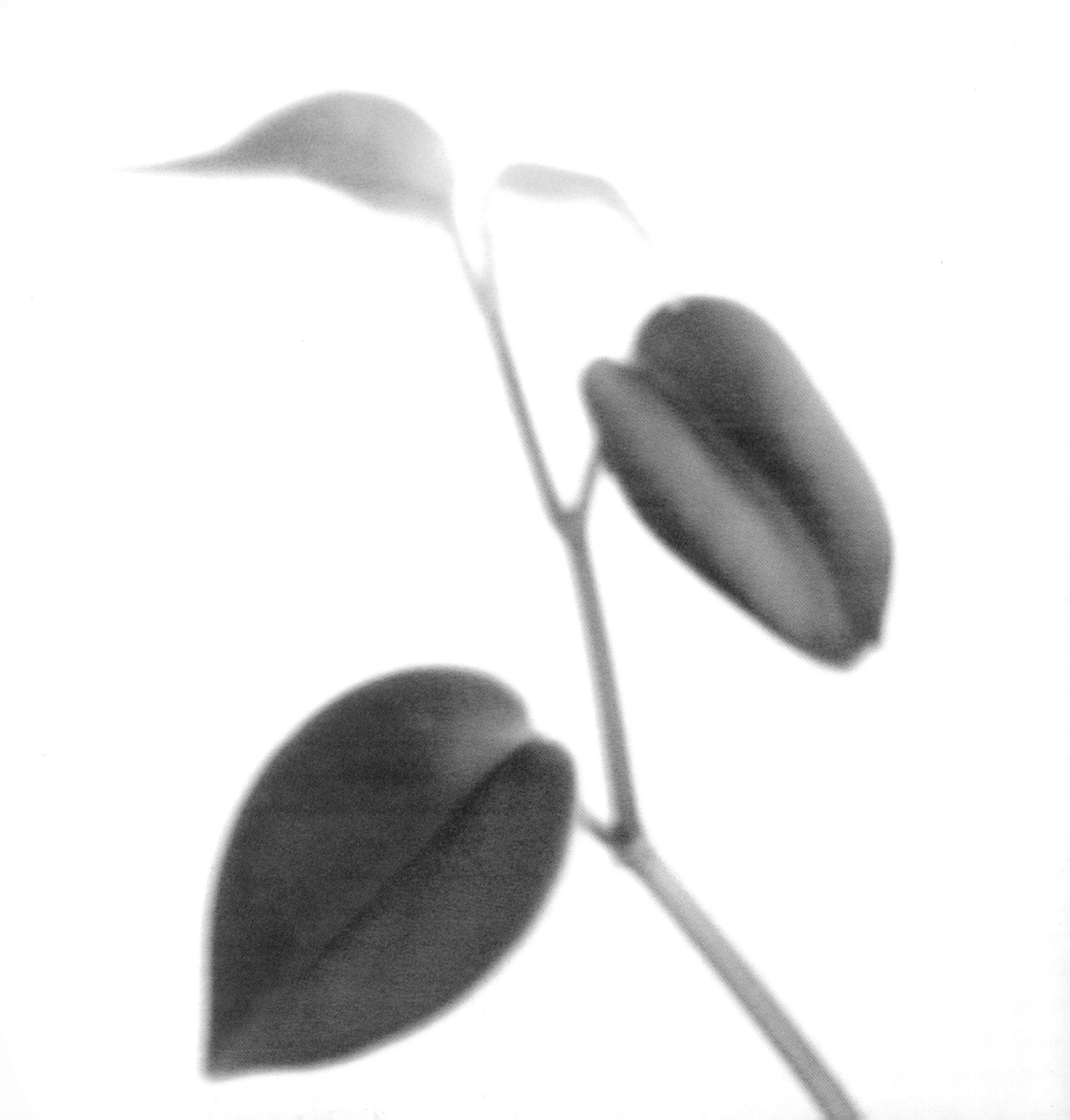

Such times,
born to Tchaikovsky's guns
that could not drown
his whispering heart.

Such times,
that closed
with our first
faltering steps
to liberty...

And I marched
as I loved, my dear,
with thee,
always with thee.

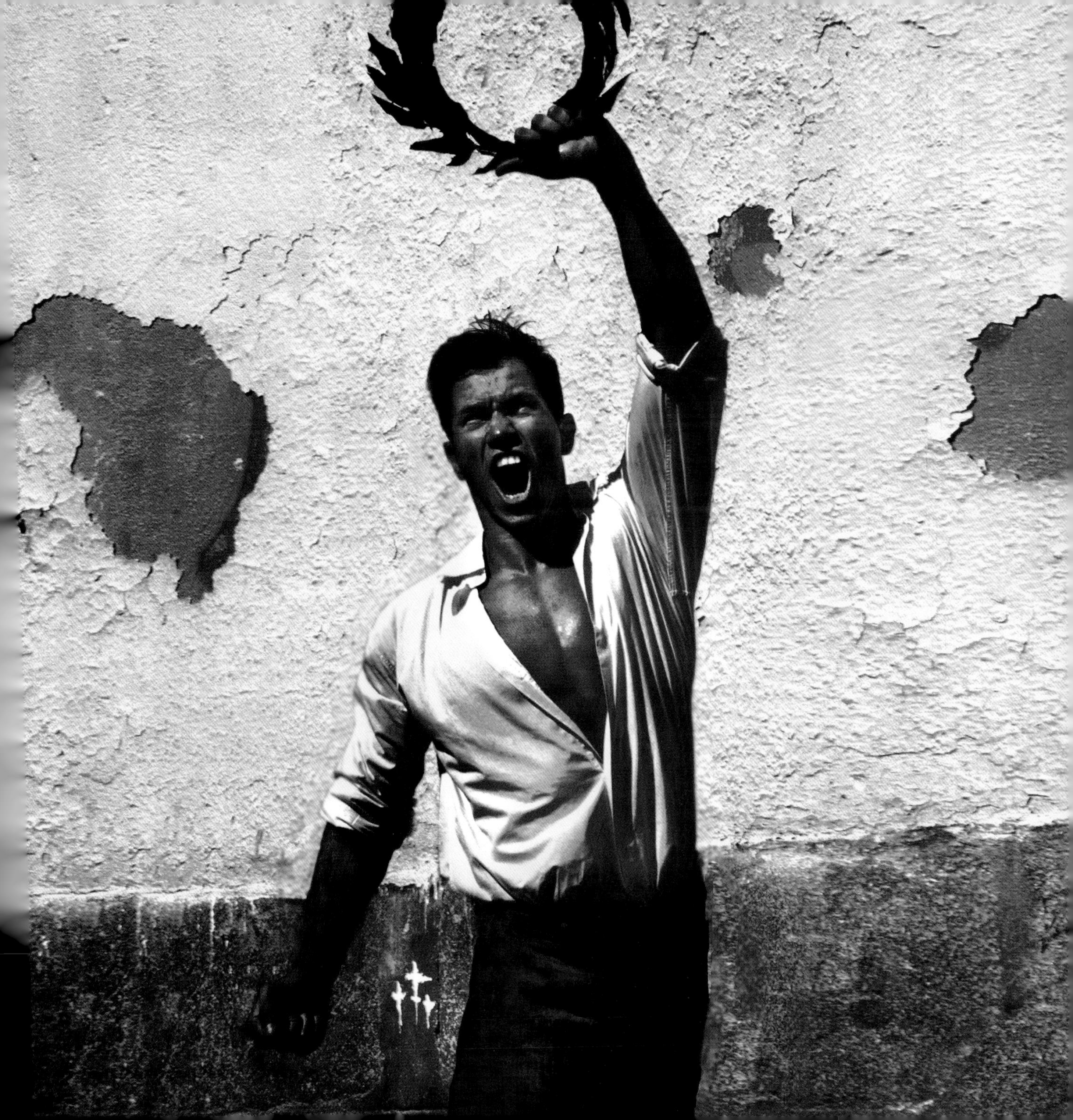

Dignity marched
abreast with shame.

Disqualified from open love
we rendezvoused in squalor,
all we were allowed.

Our culture
embracing Colette,
writing so perfectly
with Missy's name
upon her anklet,
also came to know
dark hallways;
reeking lavatories,
reminded in our tenderness
of our equivalence
with shit.

The First World War, ironically,
allowed new closeness:
young men lived
and died together
in foreign mud.

There, Wilfred Owen
gave his love a sonnet
and disk of identity,
bidding his heartbeat kiss it,
night and day,
until the name grew blurred,
fading away.

Alas, war brought
not comradeship alone,
and in defeated Germany
the crippling war-debt
was a loam where
fascist flowers
thrived horribly.

By 1933, we were already
targets of the Reich,
but still did not suspect
how far we had to fall.

In slaughterhouses,
labeled with pink triangles,
our thousands died.

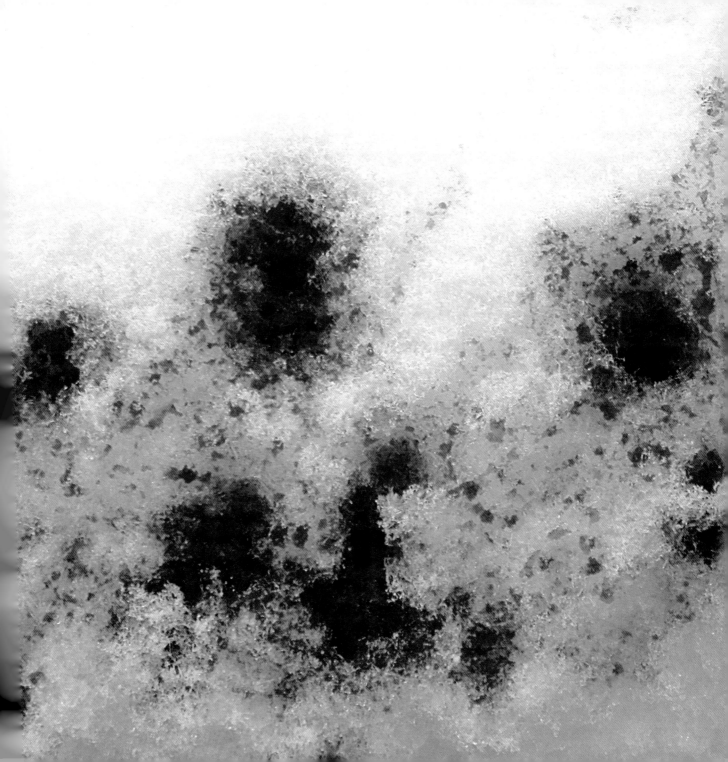

The showers, they say,
held bodies piled
as if the strong and desperate
had climbed on lovers' backs
to flee the gas,
betraying at the last
our love,
the thing we thought
they couldn't take.

Can you imagine?

Can you?

Darling, do not weep.

'Twas just a dream,
a nightmare gathered
on the century's brow,
and if it comes again
I'll hold you tight 'til dawn,
as well as I know how.

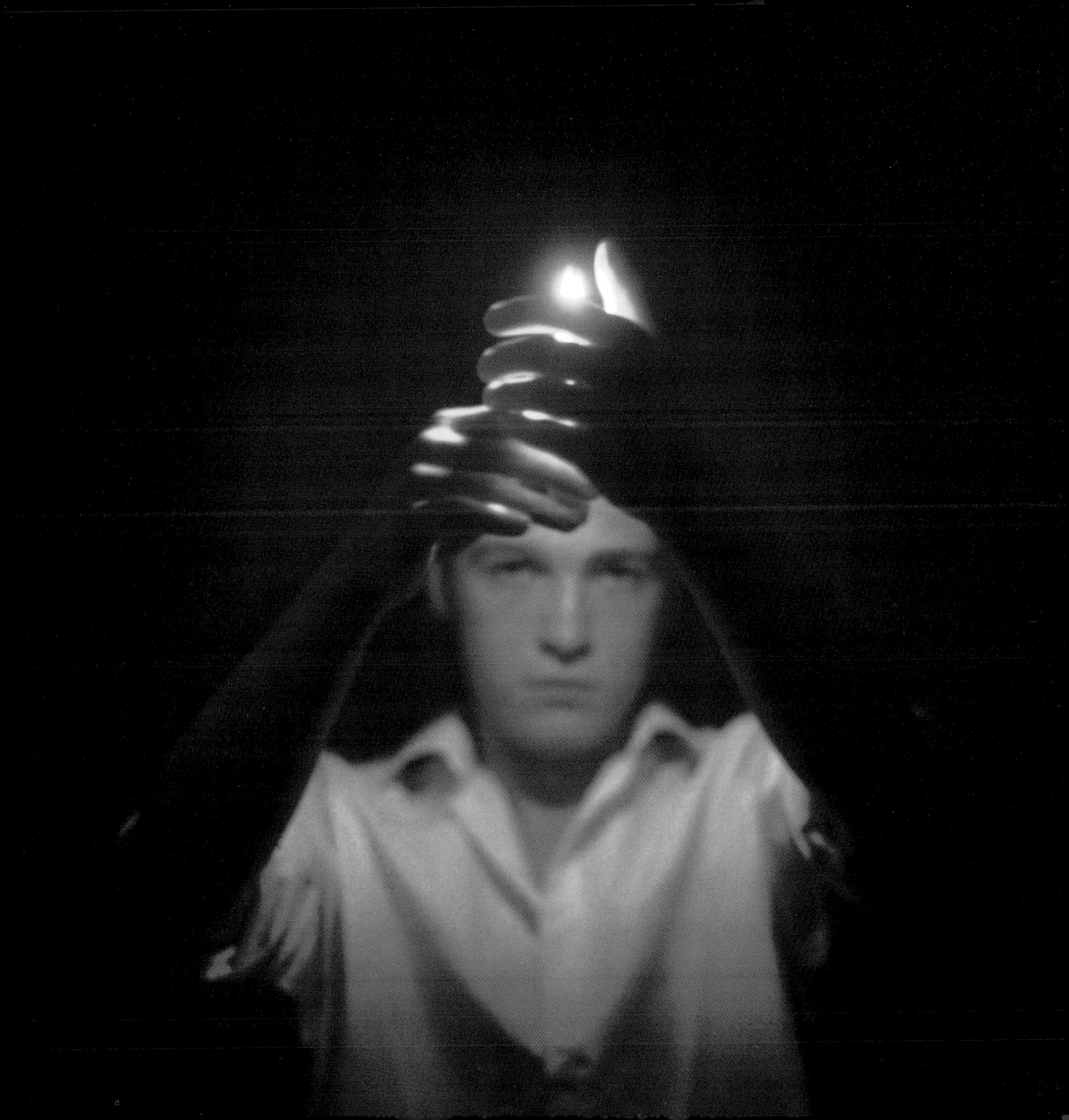

As day broke over Europe,
troops returned,
some bringing
newfound ways of life,
to settle on the Barbary Coast,
in Portsmouth
or New York.

New worlds
seemed possible,
and Ginsberg howled
against a state
that called us
communists,
not satisfied
with branding us
diseased.

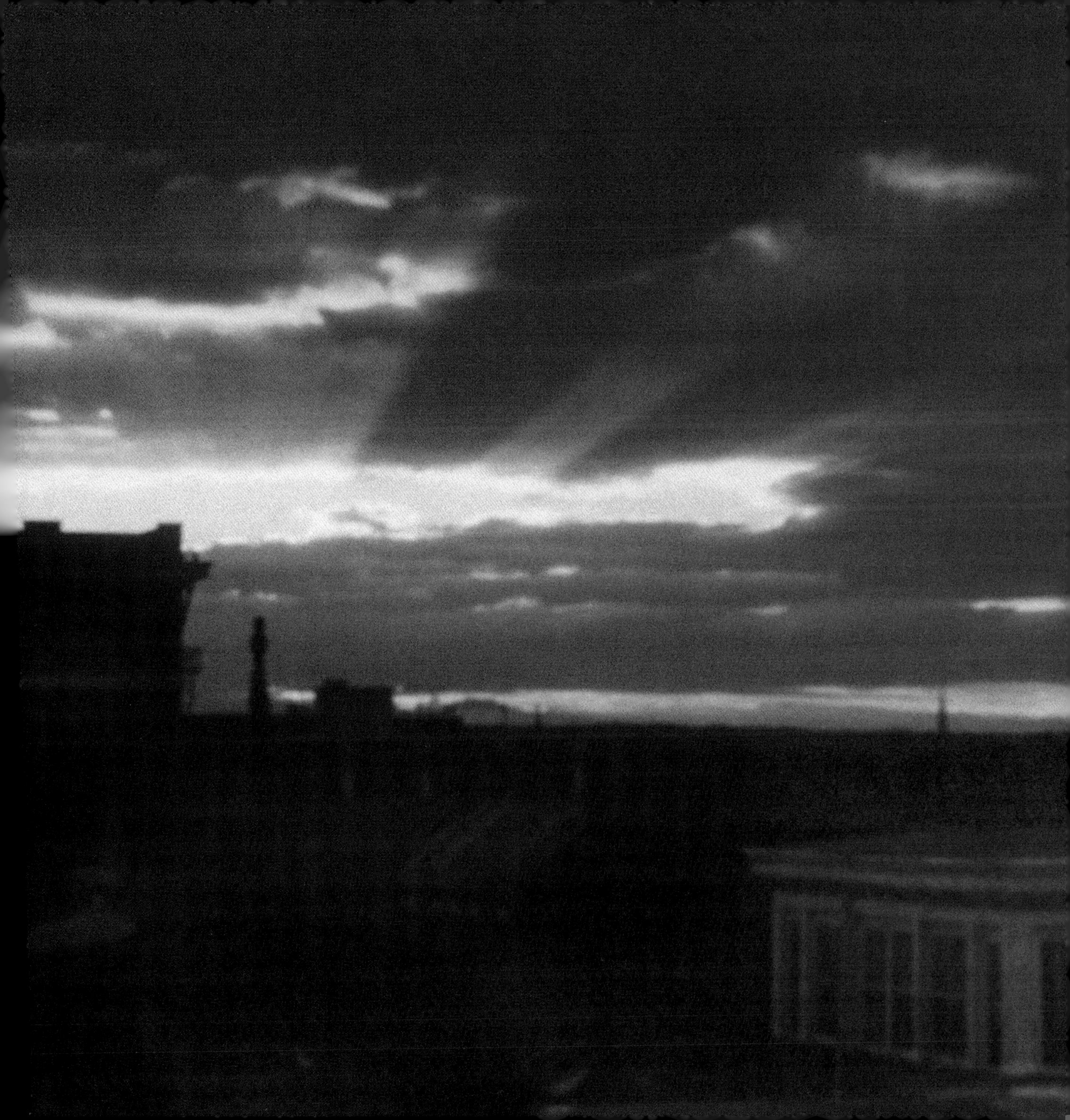

The Mattachine Society,
America's first group
for homosexual men,
was formed in 1950,
followed by
the female-oriented
Daughters of Bilitis.

Meanwhile, England
saw campaigns
for homosexual rights,
while Orton wrote
of dark young men
with new
and dangerous
moralities.

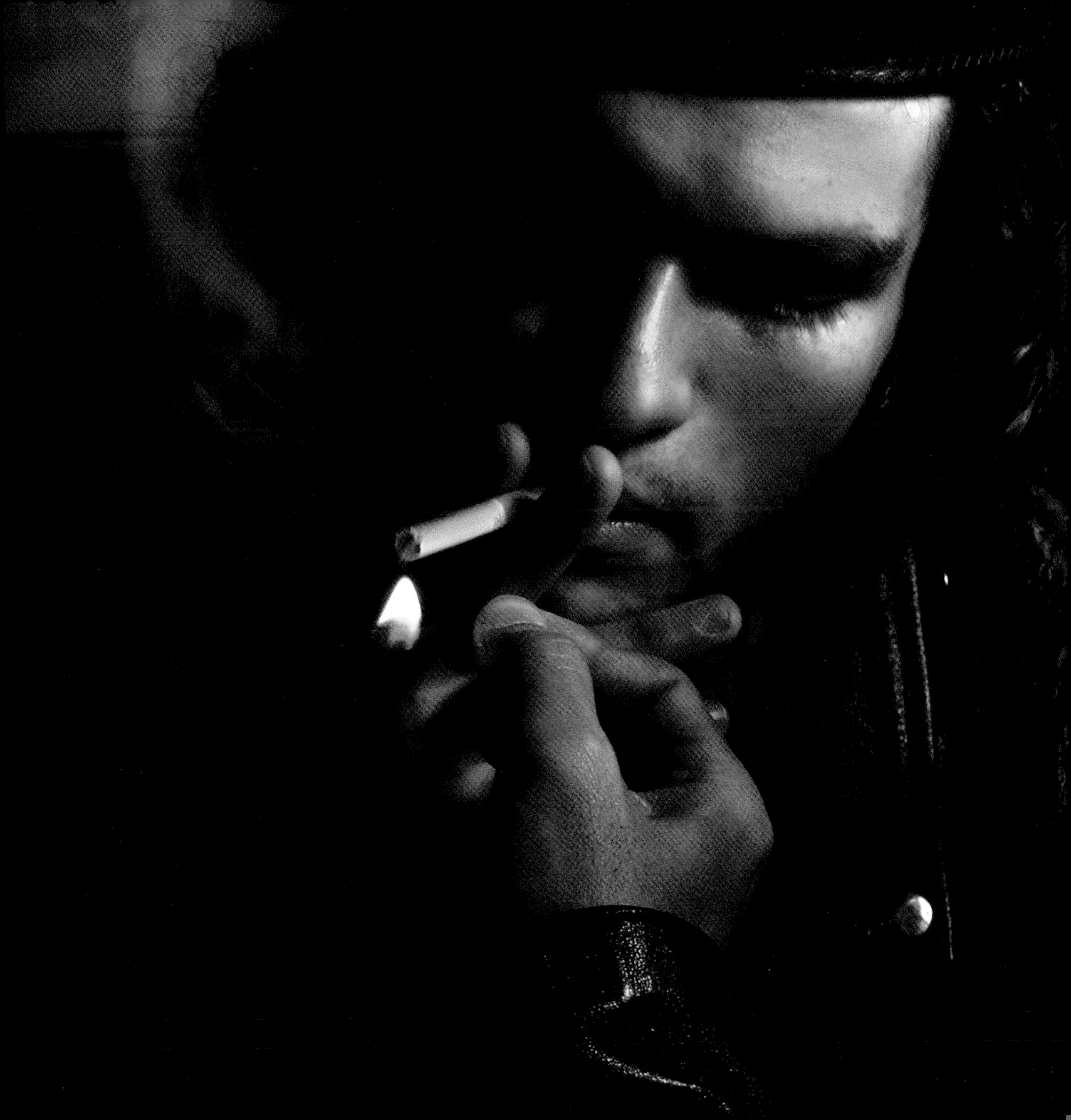

In 1967,
Britain legalized
the sexual act
between consenting
adult males,
while gradually
across America,
states came
to modify
their laws.

Though still harassed
we were yet jubilant,
the first rung
in our climb
achieved.

We splashed
in Hockney's pools
and danced
to Brian Epstein's band.

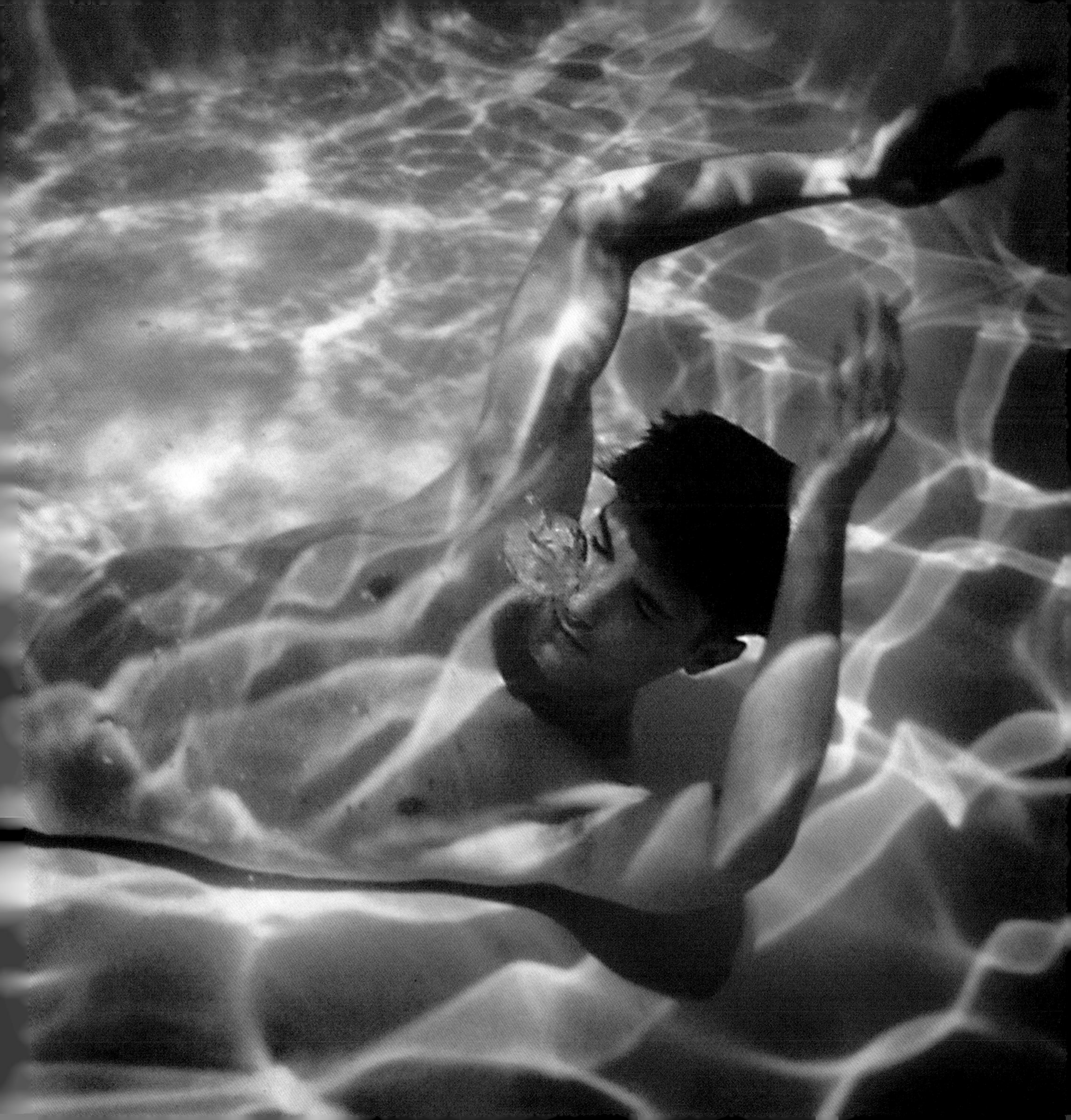

On Friday,
June the 27th, 1969,
routine police raids
on the Stonewall Inn bar
in Greenwich Village
sparked the riots
from which
Gay Liberation
sprang.

Did Judy Garland's death
or did five thousand
years of history
propel us
through the streets
and with our anger
fire the night?

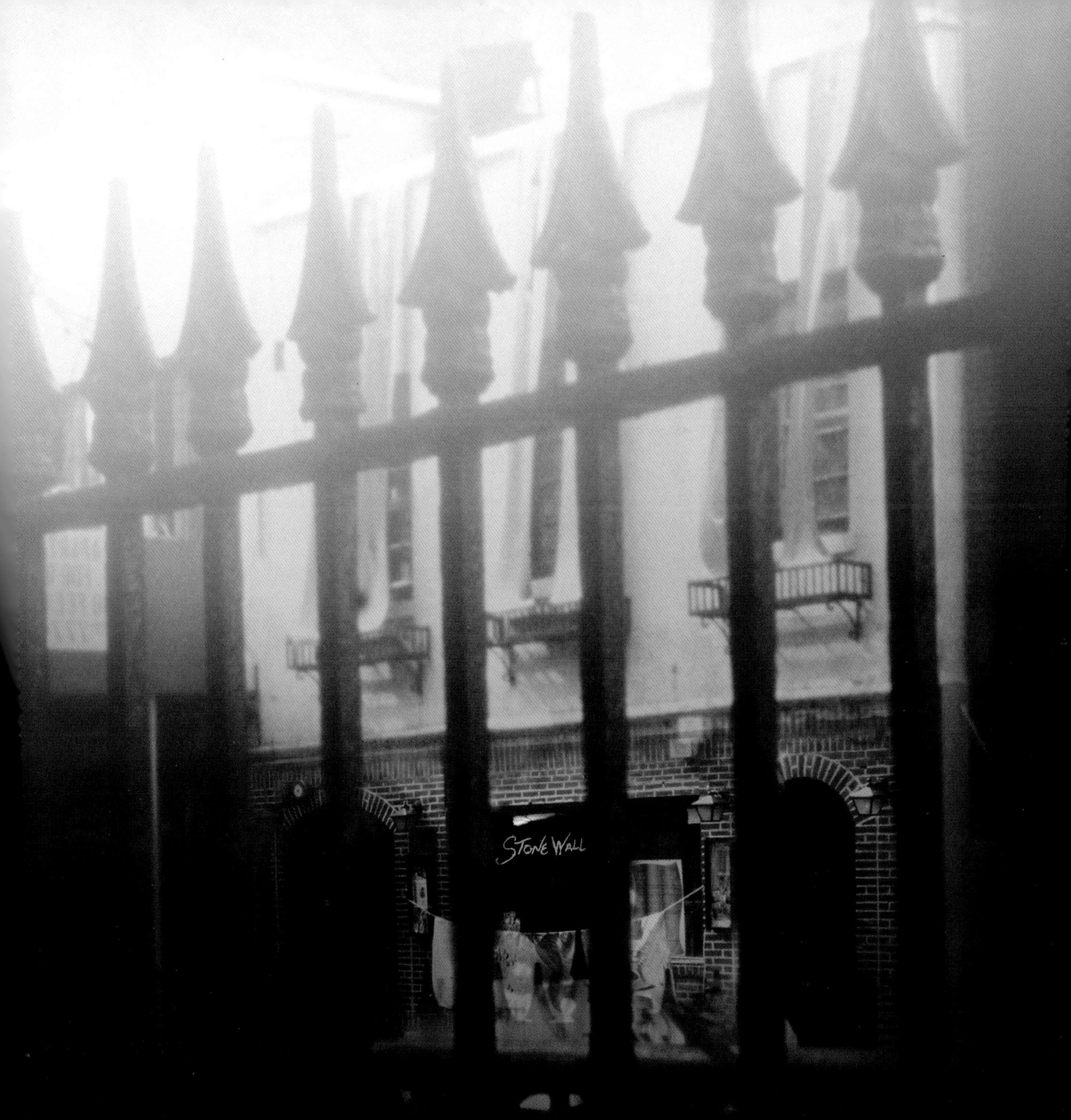
STONE WALL

Remember running
in between
the blazing trashcans
holding hands,
laughing above the sirens,
unafraid and pure?

We knew
that freedom
could be won,
that nothing
could prevent it.

We were sure, my love.

We were so sure.

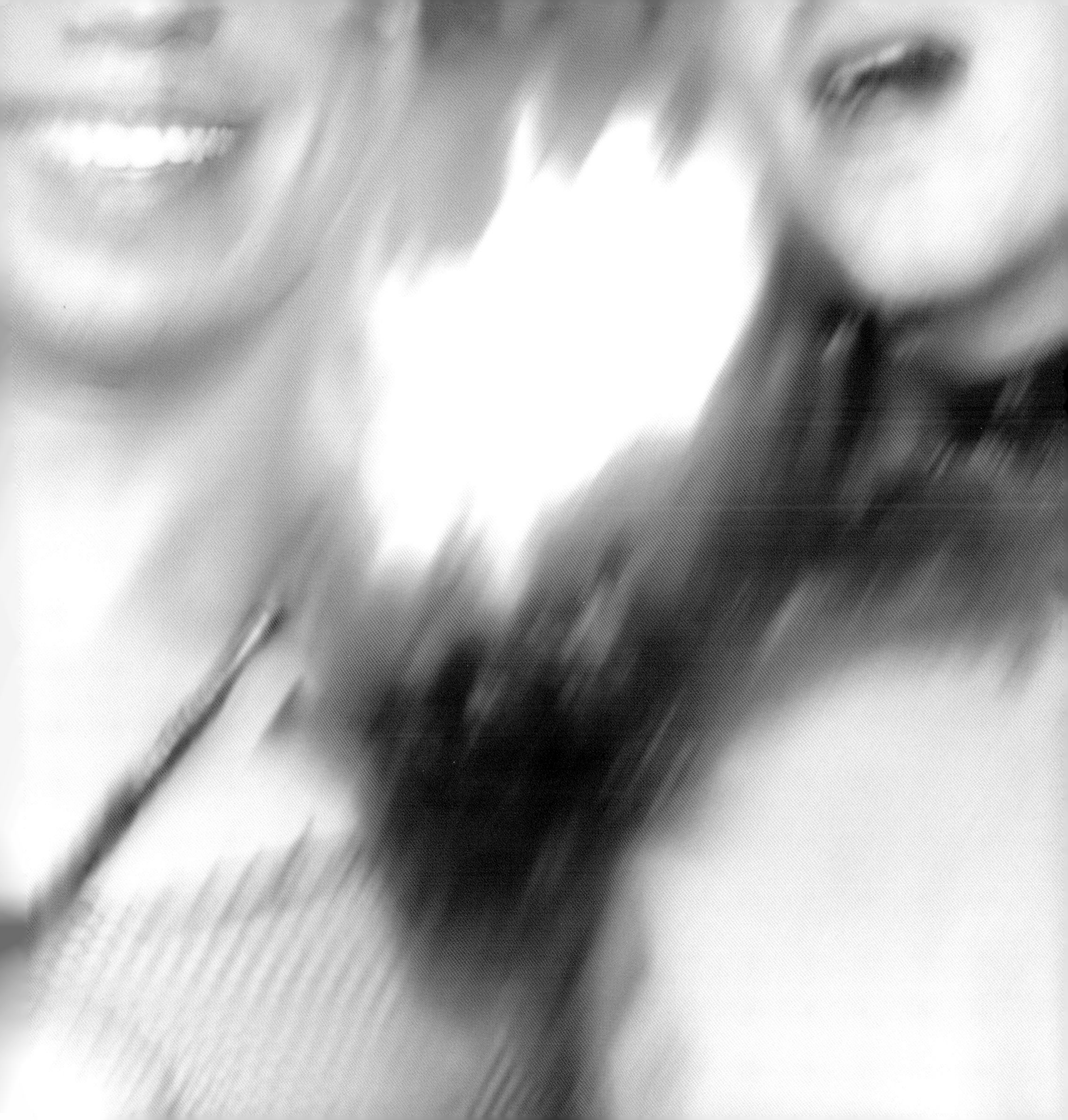

That was before the virus.

AIDS changed everything.

Though first
affecting heterosexuals,
who comprise nine-tenths
of those afflicted worldwide,
church and press spoke
of a 'gay plague.'

And we, so close
to being recognized
as fully human were,
instead, transformed
to medieval bogeymen.

A human tragedy
thus licensed human bigotry.

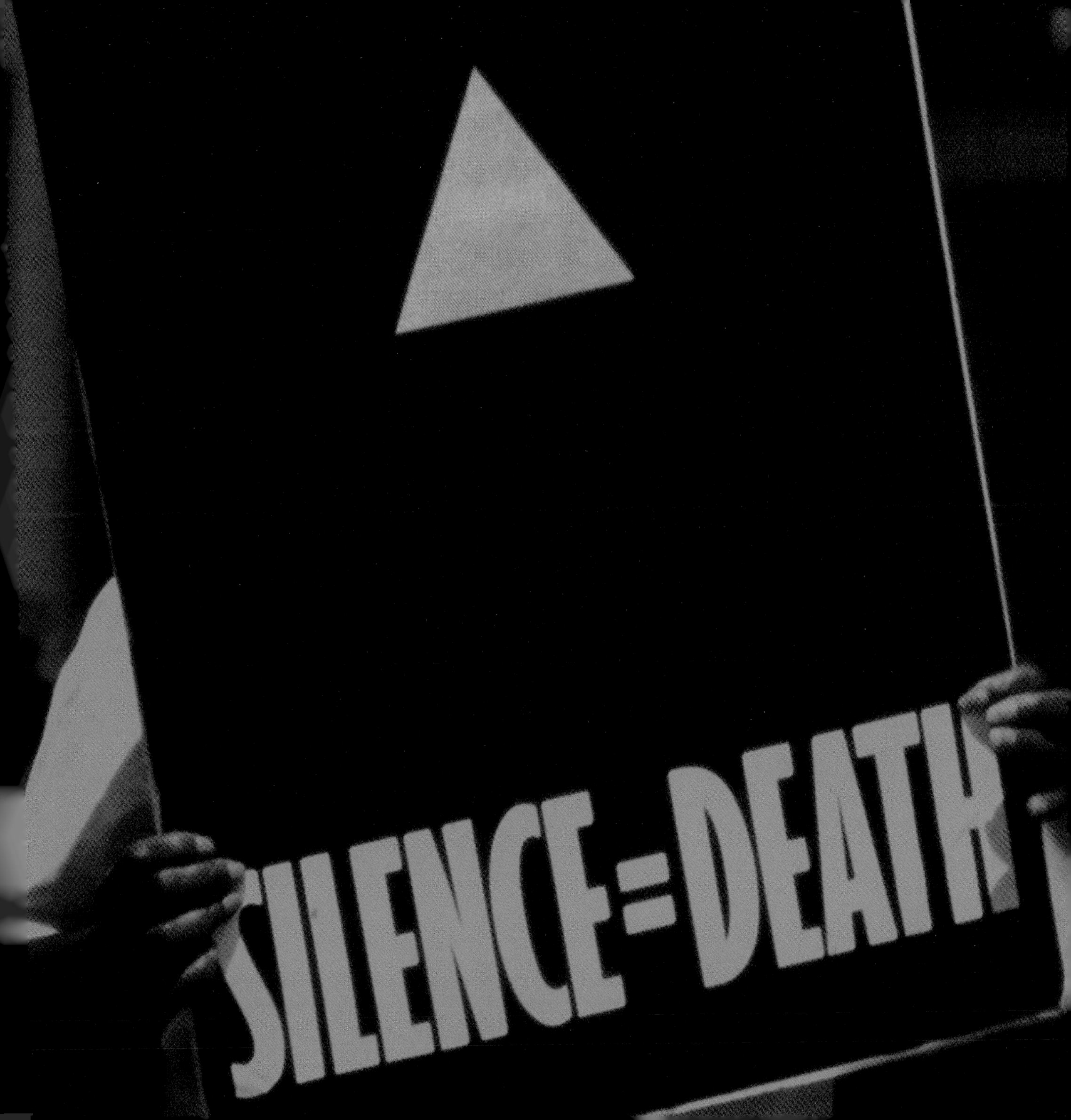
SILENCE=DEATH

Policemen claimed
to speak for God,
describing persons
having AIDS
as swilling in
a self-made cesspit,
while Councillor Brownhill,
a conservative,
recalled an earlier
final solution,
offering to
'gas the queers.'

And Margaret Thatcher
praised their forthrightness.

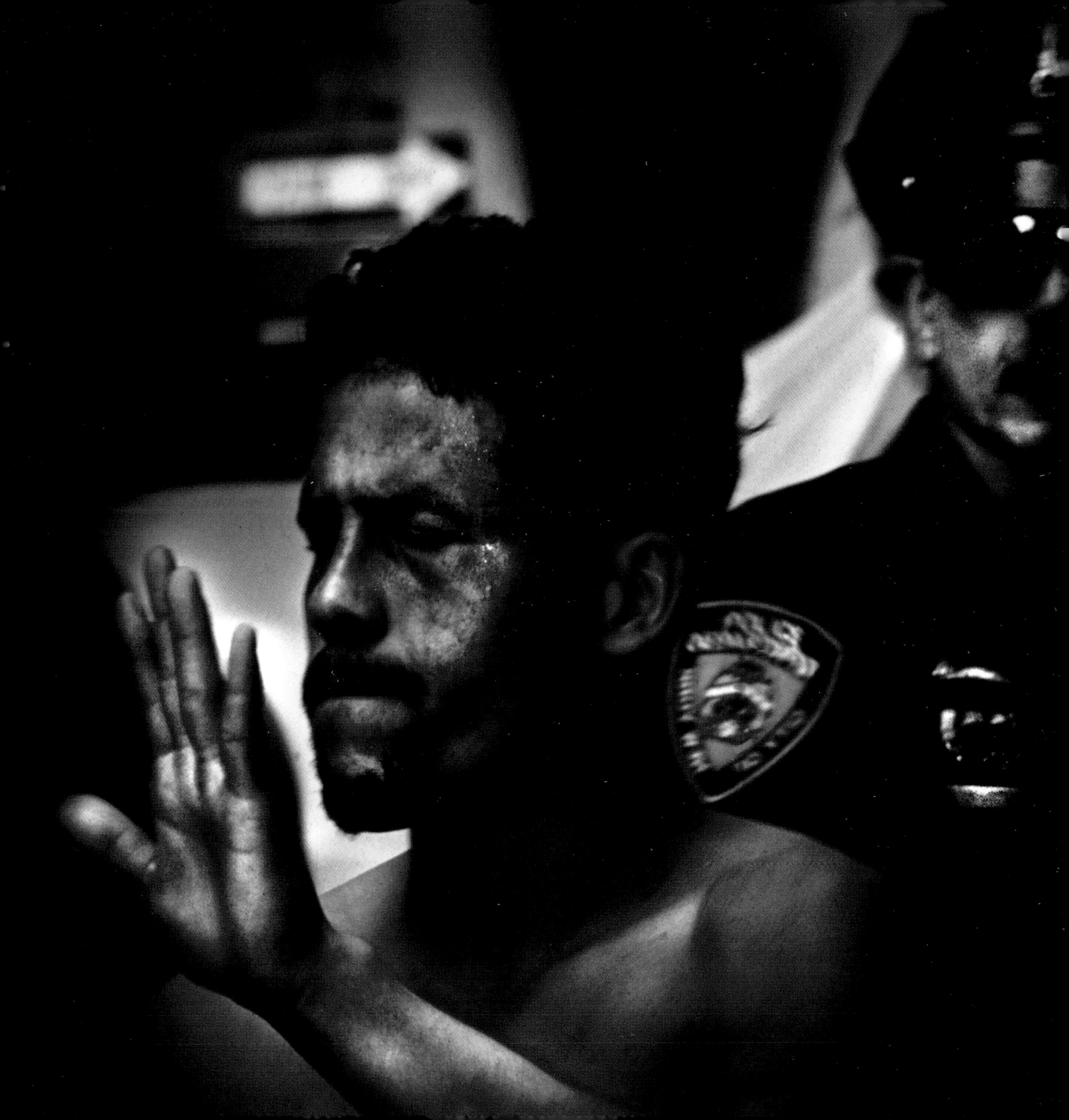

She let a clause
pass into law
that her chief minister
for local government
described as
being aimed
at banishing
all trace
of homosexuality:
the act itself,
all gay relationships,
even the abstract concept
would be gone,
a word torn
from the dictionary.

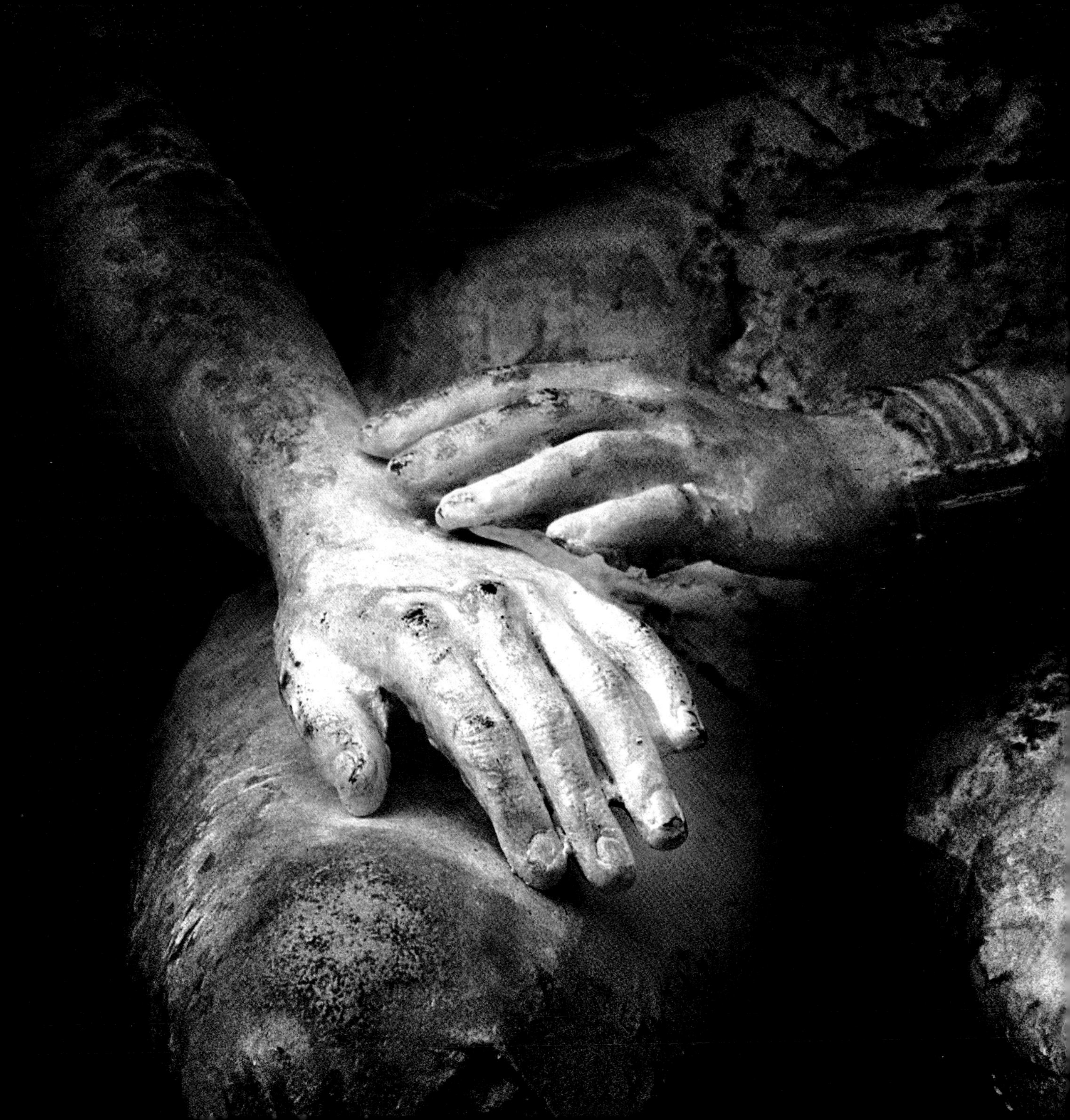

Shall we be scapegoats
as they used the Templars,
Canaanites and Jews,
or will AIDS force
abandonment of prejudice,
of furtive silence over sex,
to save their very lives?

As we approach
the future,
will Utopia's spires
hove into view,
or death-camp
chimney stacks?

My love,
I wish I knew.

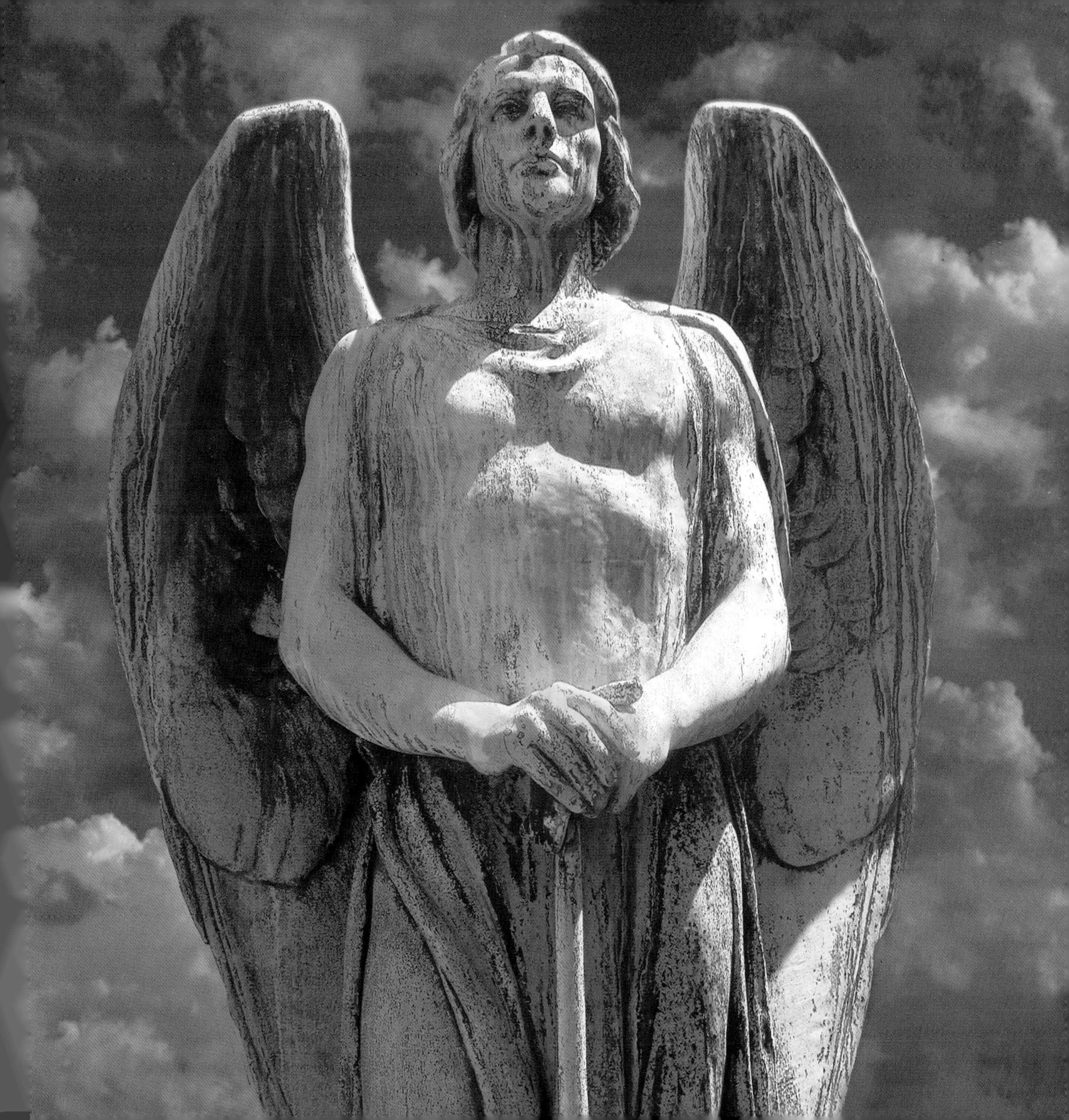

While life endures we'll love,
and afterwards,
if what they say is true,
I'll be refused a Heaven
crammed with popes,
policemen, fundamentalists,
and burn instead,
quite happily,
with Sappho, Michelangelo
and you, my love.

I'd burn throughout eternity
with you.

Appendix 1: Who's Who in *The Mirror of Love* (in order of appearance)

Urukagina's Code (p. 6)

King Urukagina of Sumer was the author of the earliest known law code(c. 2350 B.C.). The code confirmed that the "king was appointed by the gods." Among other decrees, Urukagina's Code prescribed monogamy for women and sought to enforce female fidelity by levying adultery with the penalty of death.

> "The woman who was seized by saying something to a man which she should not have said must have her teeth crushed with burnt bricks upon which her guilty deed has been inscribed."

The Books of Leviticus and Exodus (pp.6, 8)

Leviticus and Exodus are two of the five books of the Torah. Leviticus prescribes that men who have sexual contact with other men shall be put to death:

> Leviticus 18:22
>
> "Thou shalt not lie with mankind, as with womankind: it is abomination."

> 20:13
>
> "If a man also lie with mankind, as he lieth with a woman, both of them have committed an abomination: they shall surely be put to death; their blood shall be upon them."

In Exodus 22:29-30 God demands the sacrifice of the firstborn animals and children:

29

"Thou shalt not delay to offer the first of thy ripe fruits, and of thy liquors: the firstborn of thy sons shalt thou give unto me."

30

"Likewise shalt thou do with thine oxen, and with thy sheep: seven days it shall be with his dam; on the eighth day thou shalt give it me."

Homer (c. 850 B.C.) (p. 16)

Greek poet. There is consensus among modern scholars that Homer wrote both of his masterpieces, *The Iliad* and *The Odyssey*, by working from previous sources. Narrating an episode in the Trojan War, book 23 of *The Iliad* recounts the appearance of the ghost of Patroclus, the deceased beloved of Achilles, and Achilles' longing to hold him:

"Dear friend, why have you come to me here
telling me everything I need to do?
I'll carry out all these things for you,
attend to your request. But come closer.
Let's hold each other, one short moment more,
enjoying a shared lament together.

but he grasped nothing. The spirit had departed
going underground, like vapour, muttering faintly."

(Translation by Ian Johnston)

Sappho (c. 612 B.C) (pp. 16, 20, 80)

Greek poet. Sappho was born on the Greek isle of Lesbos, from which the term "lesbian" is derived. At the instigation of Pope Gregory Nazianzen, Christians burned many of her books in 380 A.D., and in 1073 A.D. a second book burning by Pope Gregory VII may have destroyed what remained of her work. Today she is preserved only in fragments, as citations in the works of classical scholars and on strips of papyrus found in Egypt.

Saint Paul (died A.D. 67) (p. 18)

Christian religious leader. Born in Tarsus (now part of Turkey), the primary sources for his life are the New Testament's Acts of the Apostles and Pauline Epistles. A onetime persecutor of Christians, St. Paul's conversion to the faith did not temper his ire when commenting on matters of chastity and sex:

Romans 1:26-27

"Because of this, God gave them over to shameful lusts. Even their women exchanged natural relations for unnatural ones. In the same way the men also abandoned natural relations with women and were inflamed with lust for one another. Men committed indecent acts with other men, and received in themselves the due penalty for their perversion."

I Corinthians 6:9-10

"Know ye not that the unrighteous shall not inherit the kingdom of God? Be not deceived: neither fornicators, nor idolaters, nor adulterers, nor effeminate, nor abusers of themselves with mankind, nor thieves, nor covetous, nor drunkards, nor revilers, nor extortioners, shall inherit the kingdom of God."

Saint Thomas Aquinas (1225–74) (p. 22)

Italian philosopher and theologian. Known as the Angelic Doctor, St. Thomas is the greatest figure of Scholasticism, one of the principal saints of the Roman Catholic Church, and founder of the system declared by Pope Leo XIII to be the official Catholic philosophy. In his discourses, he refers to the teachings of St. Paul:

"The venereal act is rendered unbecoming through being contrary to right reason, and because, in addition, it is contrary to the natural order of the venereal act as becoming to the human race: and this is called the unnatural vice. This may happen by copulation with an undue sex, male with male, or female with female, as the Apostle states (Rom. i. 27): and this is called the vice of sodomy." [Summa Theologica, Vol IV, Pt. II-II, Q.154 Art. 11]

King Philip IV (1268–1314) (p. 24)

King of France. Following the brief pontificate of Benedict XI, Philip secured the election of **Clement V** to the papacy. Together they persecuted the **Knights Templar**, an international military order formed during the Crusades, whose wealth Philip appropriated to finance his wars.

Michelangelo Buonarroti (1475–1564) (pp. 26-30, 80)

Italian sculptor, architect, painter, and poet. Born in Caprese, Michelangelo is best known for the frescoes of the Sistine Chapel in the Vatican and the statue of David in Florence. At the age of 57 he met and fell in love with a young Roman nobleman named **Tommaso de'Cavalieri**, who became his faithful companion until his death and to whom he dedicated several passionate poems.

William Shakespeare (1564–1616) (pp. 32, 40)

English playwright and poet. Born in Stratford-on-Avon, Shakespeare's sonnets are by far his most significant non dramatic works. The first 126 of the 154 poems are addressed to a young man whose identity has long intrigued scholars (See Oscar Wilde's short story "The Portrait of Mr. W. H."). In the dedication to the first edition, the publisher of the sonnets, Thomas Thorpe, claimed a person with the initials **W. H.** had served as inspiration for the poems.

The Ladies of Llangollen: Lady Eleanor Butler (1739–1829) and **Sarah Ponsonby** (1755–1831) (pp. 36, 40)

Irish gentlewomen. They fled to Plas Newydd, Llangollen, Wales, where they lived in "romantic friendship" for fifty years. Well-versed in politics and the arts, the Ladies of Llangollen often entertained poets, including **William Wordsworth**, and students of science who traveled to Plas Newydd to discuss the matters of the day.

Emily Dickinson (1830–86) (pp. 38, 40)

American poet. Born, resided, and died in the Homestead, a house built by her grandfather in Amherst, Massachusetts. Never married, Dickinson cared for her parents in their later years and was a companion to her sister, Lavinia, who also remained at the Homestead for her entire life.

Walt Whitman (1819–92) (p. 38)

American poet. Born in West Hills, New York, Walt Whitman celebrated the liberty and nobility of the human race and honored democracy and the brotherhood of man. His poems are collected in the book *Leaves of Grass*.

Natalie Barney (1876–1972) (p. 42)

American novelist, poet, and salonist. Born to a wealthy American family in Ohio, Barney began her public life when she met Oscar Wilde at the age of six. After coming out as a lesbian in the United States, she moved to Paris in 1899 and began a very pubic affair with Lilane de Pougy, a celebrated courtesan and author of romantic potboilers. Barney boasted of having "the most respectable of bad reputations," and no less than three literary works, including a novel by Colette, feature thinly-veiled portraits of her as a notorious lesbian.

Gertrude Stein (1874–1946) (p. 42)

American novelist, poet, and salonist. Born in Allegheny, Pennsylvania, Stein relocated to Paris with her lover, Alice B. Toklas, where she joined the expatriate movement. A celebrated salonist, sometimes in competition with Natalie Barney, Stein encouraged, aided, and influenced — through her patronage as well as her writing — many literary and artistic figures.

Mata Hari (Margaretha Geertruida Zelle) (1876–1917) (p. 42)

Dutch dancer and spy for Germany during World War I. Hari is known to have performed at Natalie Barney's Paris home at least twice, on one occasion dressing as Lady Godiva riding a horse adorned with emeralds.

Renée Vivien (Pauline Mary Tarn) (1877–1909) (p. 42)

English novelist and poet who wrote exclusively in French. Born in Paddington, England, she moved to Paris and changed her name to Renée Vivien as a symbol of her rebirth. While in Paris she met Natalie Barney, and the two became lovers.

Károly Mária Kertbeny (formerly **Benkert**) (1824–82) (p. 44)

German-Hungarian physician. Kertbeny coined the term *Homosexualität*, creating the word as a German cognate hybridized from the Greek *homo* (meaning same), and the Latin *sexus* (meaning sex), to refer to same-gender sexual attraction.

Oscar Wilde (1854–1900) (p. 46)

Irish playwright, novelist, and poet. In addition to courting the available young men in his social circle, Wilde frequented male brothels where he boasted that he was "feasting with panthers" ("De Profundis"). In 1891, Wilde was intimate with Lord Alfred Douglas, and Douglas's father, **John Sholto Douglas**, the eighth **Marquis of Queensbury**, accused Wilde of practicing homosexuality. After bringing action against the marquis for libel, Wilde was charged with homosexual offenses and, under England's Criminal Law Amendment, found guilty and sentenced to two years in prison. His experiences there inspired his most famous poem, "The Ballad of Reading Gaol."

Peter Ilyich Tchaikovsky (1840–93) (p. 50)

Russian composer. Tchaikovsky wed in 1877 in a disastrous attempt to cover up his homosexuality. A few days after he conducted the première of his Sixth Symphony, or *Symphonie pathétique*, he died, reportedly of cholera, though the circumstances of his death were mysterious.

Colette (**Sidonie Gabrielle Claudine**) (1873–1954) (p. 52)

French novelist. Colette had a six-year liaison with the Marquise de Belboeuf, known as Missy, and would appear at the Sapphic banquets of the day wearing a tuxedo and anklet engraved with the words, "I belong to Missy."

Wilfred Owen (1893–1918) (p. 54)

English poet. Born in Oswestry, Shropshire, Owen joined the military in 1915 during World War I and was sent to the front in 1917 as an officer with the Manchester Regiment. The horrors he endured while fighting in bitter winter conditions near the Somme — experiences he described as "seventh hell" — were the inspiration for some of his greatest poems. Owen died at the age of twenty-five, only one week before the end of the war.

The Third Reich (pp. 56-8)

Heinrich Himmler was the Reich Leader of the SS, head of the Gestapo and the Waffen-SS, and Minister of the Interior. In 1936 he created the Reich Central Office for the Combating of Homosexuality and Abortion. Under Himmler, prosecution of homosexuals peaked from 1937-39, with the police conducting raids on meetings places, seizing address books from arrested men to identify and locate other homosexuals, and establishing networks of informers to compile names that would lead to further arrests. By 1945, an estimated 100,000 men were arrested, of which some 50,000 officially defined homosexuals — a status designated by a pink triangle — were sentenced. As many as 15,000 of these men were sent to concentration camps, with the remainder serving their sentences in more standard penal institutions. It is unknown how many of these men died while imprisoned. Himmler was captured after the war, but committed suicide before going to trial in May 1945.

Allen Ginsberg (1926–97) (p. 62)

American poet. An outspoken member of the beat generation, Ginsberg is best known for "Howl" (1956), a long poem attacking American values of the 1950s.

The Mattachine Society (p. 64)

The Mattachine or Matachine Society was a gay-rights group founded in Los Angeles in 1950, named after the *Société Mattachine* from medieval and Renaissance France. The *Société* consited of masked performers, and the Society chose their name as a symbol of the hidden lives of gay men.

The Daughters of Bilitis (p. 64)

The first national lesbian organization. Founded by Phyllis Lyon and Del Martin, the Daughters of Bilitis took their name from the book *Les Chansons de Bilitis* by Pierre Louÿs, a collection of poems written in immitation of Sappho. From its modest, eight-member beginning in 1955, the Daughters of Bilitis grew into a major force, bringing lesbians together, documenting their lives, and promoting civil rights.

Joe Orton (1944–67) (p. 64)

English playwright. Orton rose to fame in London during the swinging 'sixties with plays like *Loot* and the since-filmed *Entertaining Mr. Sloane*. He also worked with gay Beatles manager Brian Epstein on producing a film about the group. Orton met a savage end in 1967 at the hands of his lover, Kenneth Halliwell.

David Hockney (1937–) (p. 66)

English painter, photographer, and printmaker. Hockney developed a highly personal realistic painting style, producing images saturated with color, pattern, and vitality. His longtime residence in Southern California also informs much of his work, such as his many joyous paintings of swimmers in undulating, light-struck pools, several of which feature his then-lover, Peter Schlesinger (See film *A Bigger Splash*).

Brian Epstein (1934–67) (p. 66)

English pop music impresario. Beginning in 1961, Epstein managed the Beatles to stardom until his tragic death from a drug overdose in 1967.

Judy Garland (1922–69) (p. 68)

American singer and film actress. The patron saint of gay camp, Garland's rise to fame as Dorothy in *The Wizard of Oz* sowed the seeds of a gay following that would continue to grow throughout her later years as a solo performer. On June 27, 1969, the same week as Garland's death, New York City police officers raided the Stonewall Inn, a Greenwich Village gay bar. Contrary to expectations, the patrons fought back, resulting in three nights of rioting that were punctuated by the appearance of "gay power" slogans on area buildings. Almost overnight, a massive grassroots gay liberation movement was born.

Baroness Margaret Hilda Roberts Thatcher (1925–) (p. 74)

English politician. Great Britain's first woman Prime Minister who promoted a "return to Victorian values." Under her government, in December 1986, the leader of South Staffordshire Council, **Councillor William Frank Brownhill**, proposed on the record that ninety percent of gay men should be exterminated in gas chambers. Meanwhile, Police Chief James Anderton said on BBC Radio 4's Sunday program that "divine inspiration" told him that people with AIDS were "swirling around in a cesspit of their own making."

Appendix II: Poems quoted in *The Mirror of Love*

I have not had one word from her

Frankly I wish I were dead.
When she left, she wept

a great deal; she said
to me, 'This parting must be
endured, Sappho. I go unwillingly.'

I said, 'Go, and be happy
but remember (you know
well) whom you leave shackled by love

'If you forget me, think
of our gifts to Aphrodite
and all the loveliness that we shared

ʹall the violet tiaras,

braided rosebuds, dill and

crocus twined around your young neck

ʹmyrrh poured on your head

and on soft mats girls with

all that they most wished for beside them

ʹwhile no voices chanted

choruses without ours,

no woodlot bloomed in spring without song…ʹ

Sappho — Translated by Mary Barnard

From thy fair face I learn, O my loved lord,
that which no mortal tongue can rightly say;
the soul, imprisoned in her house of clay,
holpen by thee, to God hath often soared:

and though the vulgar, vain, malignant horde
attribute what their grosser wills obey,
yet shall this fervent homage that I pay,
this love, this faith, pure joys for us afford.

Lo, all the lovely things we find on earth,
resemble for the soul that rightly sees
that source of bliss divine which gave us birth:

nor have we first-fruits or remembrances
of heaven elsewhere. Thus, loving loyally,
I rise to God, and make death sweet by thee.

Michelangelo Buonarroti — Translated by J. A. Symonds

1

Her breast is fit for pearls,
But I was not a 'Diver' —
Her brow is fit for thrones
But I have not a crest.
Her heart is fit for home —
I — a Sparrow — build there
Sweet twigs and twine
My perennial nest.

2

Her sweet weight on my Heart a Night
Had scarcely deigned to lie —
When, stirring, for Beliefs delight,
My bride had slipped away —

If `twas a Dream — made solid — just
The Heaven to confirm —
Or if Myself were dreamed of Her —
The power to presume —

With Him remain — who unto Me —
Gave — even as to All —
A Fiction superseding Faith —
By so much — as `twas real —

Emily Dickinson

I Dream'd in a dream, I saw a city invincible to the attacks of the whole of the rest of the earth;

I dream'd that was the new City of Friends;
Nothing was greater there than the quality of robust love—it led the rest;
It was seen every hour in the actions of the men of that city,
And in all their looks and words.

Walt Whitman

Sonnet to My Friend, with an Identity Disk

If ever I had dreamed of my dead name
High in the heart of London, unsurpassed
By Time for ever, and the Fugitive, Fame,
There seeking a long sanctuary at last, —

Or if I onetime hoped to hide its shame,
— Shame of success, and sorrow of defeats, —
Under those holy cypresses, the same
That shade always the quiet place of Keats,

Now rather thank I God there is no risk
Of gravers scoring it with florid screed.
Let my inscription be this soldier's disc.
Wear it, sweet friend. Inscribe no date nor deed.
But may thy heart-beat kiss it, night and day,
Until the name grow blurred and fade away.

Wilfred Owen

Appendix III: Suggested Readings

Homosexuality in History by Colin Spencer (Harcourt Brace and Company)
When Alan Moore decided to write *The Mirror of Love* over a decade ago, he headed for the local library and looked for the "Big Book Of Gay History," which did not exist at the time. *Homosexuality in History*, published in 1995, is that book. Eminently readable and concise, it covers almost the same ground as *Mirror*, but is much more expanded.

Homosexuality & Civilization by Louis Crompton (The Belknap Press of Harvard University Press)
A new, marvelous, copiously illustrated history of homosexuality that contrasts the relative tolerance of most non-Western cultures with the "hatred, contempt, and death" promoted by Judeo-Christian and Islamic traditions. A passionate, informed, and elegant chronicle of twenty-four centuries of same-sex love.

The Penguin Book of Homosexual Verse, edited by Stephen Coote (Penguin Books)
Unable to find a book on gay history, Moore decided to piece the history together through the love lives of great gay and lesbian artists. This book was his main source and remains the best reference of its kind.

Love Speaks Its Name, edited by J. D. McClatchy (Alfred A. Knopf)
Similar to the Penguin anthology, but much more concise, this small book of poems features most of the writers quoted in *Mirror*, as well as a beautiful and insightful introduction by poet J. D. McClatchy. A great gift book, even for yourself.

Pictures and Passions, A History of Homosexuality in the Visual Arts by James M. Saslow (Penguin Books)
The first comprehensive analysis of gay and lesbian art, from the Stone Age to Stonewall. A profusely illustrated and handy reference book. Winner of two Lambda Literary Awards.

A Hidden Love by Dominique Fernandez (Prestel Verlag)
A gorgeous coffee table book covering the scope of gay and lesbian history in the visual arts. By far the best book on the subject, it is insightful, comprehensive, and features crisp reproductions of nearly every significant work of visual art pertaining to the topic. Winner of a Lambda Literary Award.

And for those readers that understand Spanish:

Amores iguales. Antología de la poesia gay y lésbica (Equal Loves. An Anthology of Gay and Lesbian Poetry) by Luis Antonio de Villena (La Esfera de los Libros)
Thank God for Villena! A gifted poet himself, like McClatchy, he has put together a selection of not just the usual suspects of gay and lesbian letters, but all the important authors that wrote poetry in Spanish and other European languages. An excellent introduction to the work of Lorca, Cernuda, Fuentes, Pasolini, Fassbinder, Arenas, and over a hundred others.

Appendix IV: What Was Clause 28?

More than fifteen years after it was approved, and as this book was being completed, Clause 28 was finally repealed. This is from the website of Stonewall, the main organization that opposed the law:

Section 28 or Clause 28 are the common names for Section 2a of the Local Government Act of 1986. This section prohibited local authorities in England and Wales from "promoting" homosexuality. It also labeled gay family relationships as "pretend".

On Thursday 10 July 2003 the House of Lords voted overwhelmingly to repeal Section 28 of the Local Government Act in England and Wales. This followed a similar massive vote in the House of Commons in March.

The repeal of Section 28 had been supported by a coalition of children's organizations, teachers, school governors, local authorities, trades unions, health experts, and lesbian, gay, and bisexual groups. Almost 25,000 people across the UK signed up to Stonewall's "Let's Nail Section 28" campaign, through our online petition, in bars and clubs such as London's G.A.Y., and via postcards distributed at events, between friends, and through community networks.

To join Stonewall contact:

Stonewall
46 Grosvenor Gardens
London, SW1W 0EB UK
Phone 020-7881-9440
Fax: 020-7881-9996
info@stonewall.org.uk
http://www.stonewall.org.uk

The equivalent organization in the United States is:

Human Rights Campaign
1640 Rhode Island Ave., N.W.
Washington, D.C. 20036-3278 USA
Phone: 202-628-4160
TTY: 202-216-1572
Fax: 202-347-5323
hrc@hrc.org
http://www.hrc.org

ACKNOWLEDGEMENTS

I would like to thank Alan for writing this piece and trusting me to care for it and nurture it.

I also give heartfelt thanks to all my models, without whom this book would not have been possible: Dunia, Tomás, Fernando, John, Aleksey, Aurora, Steve, Luis, Moli, Andrés, Denis, Roman, Katsu, and Jesús. Thank you for your enthusiasm and generosity.

Thanks to George of A.T. Jones & Sons, Baltimore, for his marvelous costumes and props.

Special thanks to my mother for being my location scout, impromptu assistant, and best critic. And to my brother Álvaro for his invaluable help and advice.

Thanks to Chris and Brett for making this book possible, David and Robert for their lovely text pieces, Rob for his impeccable proofreading, François for suggesting the project in the first place, Paul for his design savvy, Melinda for the superb portrait, and Clive, Chip, Manil, David, James, and Andy for their great quotes.

And finally, thanks to all the friends and family members who gave me their support and encouragement while completing this project.

José Villarrubia
Baltimore, 2003

The images in this book were shot in the following locations: Baltimore, Daytona Beach, and New York City in the United States; London and Northampton in the United Kingdom; Paris, France; and Madrid, Spain.

For inquiries regarding limited edition prints of the images featured in this book contact the artist at TheMirrorofLove@aol.com

Detail from *The Mirror of Love* by Aubrey Beardsley, 1895.

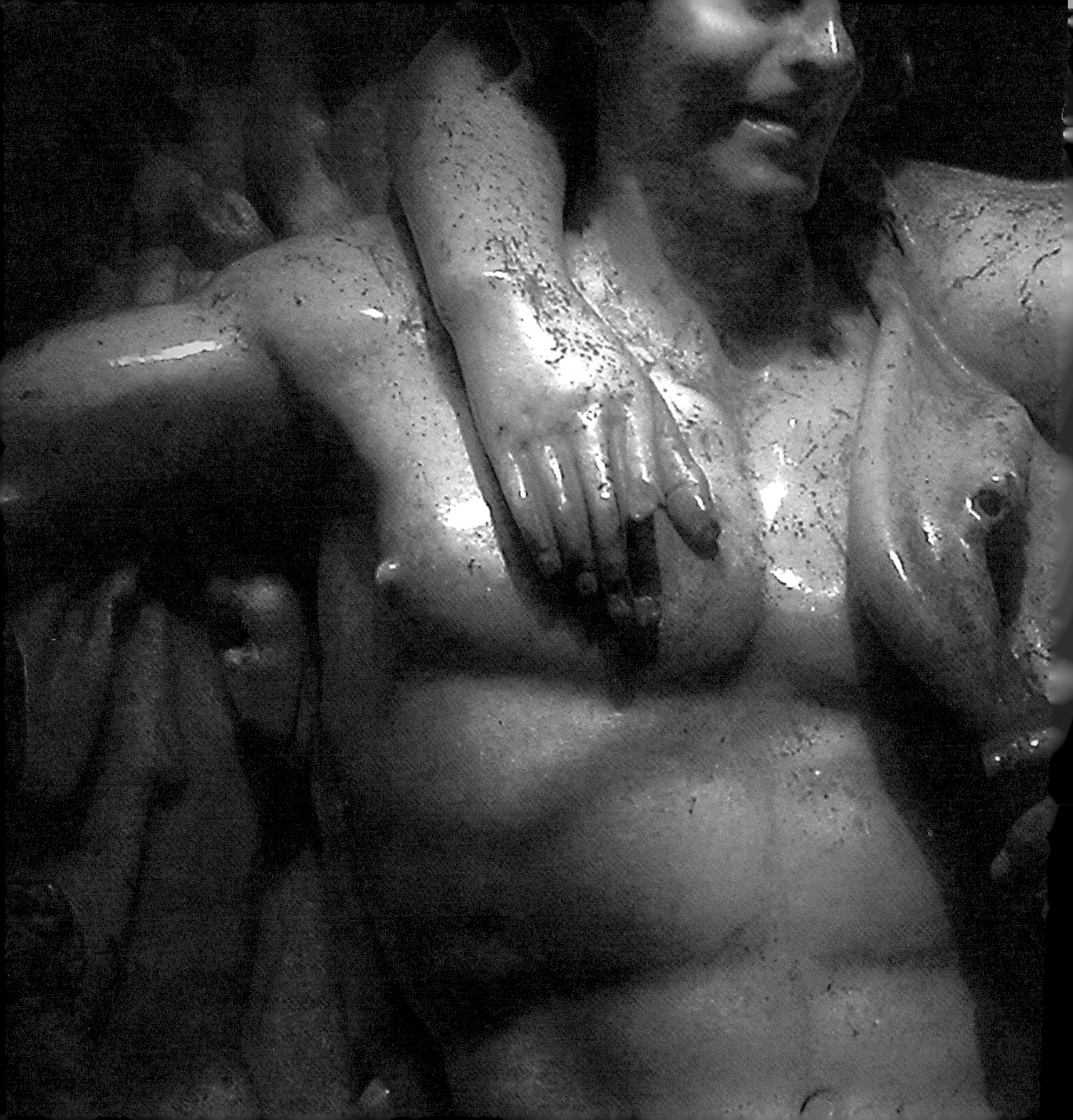